IS GOD
REAL
OR WHAT?

IS GOD REAL OR WHAT?

CURTIS PEART

TATE PUBLISHING
AND ENTERPRISES, LLC

Published by Tate Publishing & Enterprises, LLC
127 E. Trade Center Terrace | Mustang, Oklahoma 73064 USA
1.888.361.9473 | www.tatepublishing.com

Tate Publishing is committed to excellence in the publishing industry. The company reflects the philosophy established by the founders, based on Psalm 68:11,
"The Lord gave the word and great was the company of those who published it."

Book design copyright © 2012 by Tate Publishing, LLC. All rights reserved.
Cover design by Kristen Verser
Interior design by Christina Hicks

Published in the United States of America

ISBN: 978-1-61862-262-4
Religion / Christian Life / Inspirational
12.02.28

DEDICATION

To my dear mother, Zelma Peart, who loved the Lord and would not give up on her children, even in very hard times, and who was instrumental in all of her children being led to Christ.

To my father, Arnold Peart, who worked hard to feed and care for his family. To my pastor, Rev. Copland Lodge, who was such a good pastor and also powerful teacher, who fed me the word in my early Christian life.

To my dear beloved wife, Collette Peart, who stuck by me through good times and bad. To my daughter Lavinia and her husband, Tennyson Hurd, and their children, who gave me support and encouragement as I write. To my second daughter, Rowena, and her children; and to my last child, Natalie, for her support; to my church family at Trinity Faith Pentecostal Church of God for their support, and all the many friends who encourage and support me.

INTRODUCTION

As I travel the world, there seems to be this great thought that passes though the mind of man: is there really a God, or does every thing we see around us just happen by chance—the sun shining by day, set in the right space and distance from the earth to give the right climate for our existence here on earth; animals and plants; the moon shining by night that also have so much grand effect for everyone's and everything's existent; the wind, rain, hail, thunder, snow, lightening, earthquakes, and the great waters with every living and dead things in it; the small streams flowing most graciously down the hillside; the birds in the branches of the apple trees singing their happy song; the animals both great and small, just to name a few. Tell me, could it be possible that all this just happens by chance, or could there be more to this?

Could there be a designer behind all of this? It makes me think; are we not human, one great intelligent creature? Is it not true that if we want to build a house, no matter how big or how small, don't we first think of it then make a plan so that whatever we do, it will turn out right? So, let's just stop for a moment and look about us. Don't just look—*think*. Look again with everything so detailed and well put together. Doesn't it seem that some great power is behind all this?

In my earlier years, before the Lord found me, after listening to so many talk of how the world came to be, I too was led away, and I could not believe that there was a God who was watching over me. If so, I wondered, why didn't he show himself to me? If he is real and loves the world so much, then why does he allow so much people to die, some even in tragic ways: storms, earthquakes, floods, mudslides, fire, etc.? Why doesn't he come in and stop it from happening?

As I thought this over, the one thing that stood out to me was a teacher who told me that God was not real. This teacher claimed that the Bible was written by men and designed to brainwash us and keep us in slavery. He said that the Bible was designed to change the way we thought and acted which then puts us under subjection.

As you read this book, you will see how God has revealed Himself to me. This has caused me to have a change of mind. I am writing this book to show that the God we serve is very much real and not make-believe as so many think. I also will be using other peoples' personal testimony as confirmation that our God is real.

What do you think? Help me answer this question: is God real or what? When you read, you will see through the author's eyes how God was real in his life from a child to an adult. The author hopes that young people too will find hope in knowing that God is real, and when they have problems, there is someone they can look to for help.

It gives me joy to write this book, seeing that, as a pastor, I have met many people from many different nations who seem very confused about the existence of a holy, all-powerful being called Jehovah God. This seems a very hard fact to accept for many, but I hope my stories will give some insight as to why there has to be a God. You will also hear real stories in the lives of other people. You will read of others who witness His existence. Some things may seem unreal. I promise, if you find time to start reading, you might just enjoy it. As you take time to read, you will find your faith being lifted; and if you have doubt of the love of God toward you, you will be healed in mind and body. Please note, I have no intention of boring you with stories; my pure intention is to impart knowledge.

The reason for this book is to show that the God we serve is real and not as many people think Him to be a fairytale.

TABLE OF CONTENTS

THE NEED
FOR A BIGGER
HOUSE

I, Curtis Peart, was born in Jamaica, W.I., to Arnold and Thelma Peart. I was the first of ten children born to my parents. I was the second child of my father. The first was my sister, Gloria, who was born out of wedlock, and the second child for my mother, after Milton, a brother born out of wedlock. Ours was not a rich family, so both my mother and father had to work to take care of the family. My mother was a domestic worker, and my father a farmer.

Being the first child in the family really had its pay off. When I was the only child, I was treated like an angel and can still remember riding on my father's back while my father knelt down cleaning the floor. I can still hear the juggle-juggy and waddle-waddle as my parents would make fun of me. (Don't get confused with these funny words in our culture; they are some of the words that our parents would use as they played with their babies.) However, this was short lived, as another brother, Noel, was added to the family. As the family got bigger, my parents saw the need for a bigger house, so plans were made to make an addition to the existing two-room house.

I was six years old at the time and considered the big son in the family. I would help with the building of the new house, a task that did not seem too hard to a six-year-old boy. You see, the most important thing was to have the material to build with. The village women would get together to prepare food for the working men. Sometimes, preparation would begin from the night before as they would bring big pots to cook in.

They would bake pudding known by most Jamaicans as Pone, a pastry made from grated sweet potatoes, grated coconuts, sugar, water, flour, nutmeg, and vanilla for flavoring. After mixing the ingredients together, you would put it in a big pot or pan, light a fire below it and a fire on top of it, then leave it to bake. One common Jamaican phrase that was often used for this method was, "hell a top hell a bottom, hallelujah in the middle." What this really means is fire on top, fire on the bottom, but a sweet food in the middle.

As I grew up, I soon learned that the reason why baking was done this way was because the poorer families in those days did not have an oven to bake in, so they improvised.

The same thing could be done with cornmeal, banana, plantain, or yam. This pudding was a good morning meal when the men of the village came together to work, and this happens very often when a family has some big work to be done, be it farming, clearing a wooded area, or building or adding to a house. As long as there was enough work for everyone, the person with the job to be done would tell it to the friends and neighbors, and they would plan a day when they would all come together and make a big workday. One Jamaican phrase that was used for this was, "day for day," which means that you help me today, I help you tomorrow. All the person who had the work to be done had to do was make sure that there was food for all and materials for the job.

Getting the necessary materials needed for building a house can be hard work. In those days, we had to carry water on our heads for mixing the mortar and for drinking. This was hard work. Sometimes we got help from the heavens; when the rain fell, we would set buckets to catch the water. My father would also go to the maul pit, dig the maul, and carry it on his head until there was a big maul hill where the building would take place. Maul comes from a soft stone that, when mined, would come out as white sand and is usually found on hillsides. Some people would go to the maul pit, buy this material, and have it delivered to the building sites. But, in most neighborhoods you could find these pits pre-dug for those who needed to use it.

I remember when, one day after coming home from school, I decided to go to the maul pit and help carry some maul. My dad had spread a canvas sheet on the ground on which he had put some maul that was prepared for a special kind of work on the house. This was done by running the course maul through a sifter and later throwing away the hard or ruff parts. In those days, most of us kids used to go barefoot because we could not afford house shoes; all I had was one "good" pair of shoes for church and one everyday pair they nicknamed "sunflash" because it was made of plastic that would get hot in the sun and burn your feet.

On this day, I went to the maul pit barefoot with my little carrying pail to get some maul. My feet somehow got under the canvas that was spread for the maul, and suddenly, something bit me. A sudden pain rushed through my leg. I dropped the pail I was carrying and ran home as fast as I could. I cried at the top of my voice all the way home. After the pain subsided, I went back to see what it was that bit me. To my surprise, I saw that it was a scorpion. I got a piece of stick and killed it then took some maul home.

The children would help with gathering materials, but most times we would just sit around and enjoy the fun of watching the men and women at work. The children could not join in the conversations and jokes of the adults because it was considered out of order by the elders unless we were invited into a conversation by one of them. Still, we learned most of our jokes and stories during these times by watching the adults work and listening to them talk.

With everyone working so hard, it was not long that the work was finished, and we had two new rooms added to our house. We were very happy because now we had more beds added. Before, Noel and I had to sleep together on one bed, but now, other beds would be added, and I, as the eldest son, would soon get my own bed.

Even though I might seem to be very excited about this, really my brother and I sleeping on the same bed was not too much of a problem. As children growing up together, we shared almost everything, and this we did happily. What could we do? Whether we liked it or not, our parent was the boss. If we rebelled, this would be problem for us.

THESE WERE HAPPY TIMES

My childhood was a happy time. Most families did not have TV or radios in their homes, so we had to find ways to pass the time. During the days, the district was always alive with neighborhood children playing outside together. At nights, our parents would tell us stories to help us pass time. I remember the first time my father brought home a radio. We were so happy to have a radio in the house that the next day I couldn't wait to tell all my friends about this radio my father brought us; now we could have music in the house and learn from the news what was happening in other parts of the world.

Even though we didn't have plenty and life seemed poor, my childhood days were never boring, and we always had lots of fun. We always had something to eat because our land was very fertile, and we were blessed with many fruit trees such as mangos, pears, apples, oranges, and many more. We never had to worry about not having food on our table, because if we ever felt hungry we could have our pick of what we felt like eating at the moment. We could climb a fruit tree, cut a cane, or find something else to eat. Sometimes, when we were called for lunch or dinner, we were already filled. We were really blessed.

Our home was located near our school, our church, and the local store, so most of the time we could hear the school or church bell ringing. We would run down and over the hill and make it there on time, before roll call. Our church was an Anglican Church, otherwise known as the Church of England. Every Sunday, everyone would get up early, get ready, and go to church because, to us, this was the Lord's Day, and we owed it to him to be in church. When you walk into the church, you could hear a pin drop. Everyone was so quiet; these people were really obeying the scripture that said "Be still and know that I am God." As a child, I loved the Lord and my Church and was very eager to learn all I could. I was particularly curious about a box that was always closed and seemed well protected. Even though it was near to the entrance, it was in one corner and had a protection around it as if to say, "Look but don't touch."

I remember going to church one day with my cousin and asking him what this object was, pointing to the box. He responded, "This is where they keep the Holy Spirit." He went on to explain to me how important the Holy Spirit was and why we shouldn't play around or touch this object. He explained that without the Holy Spirit in the church, the church was no church at all, so every church needs the Holy Spirit to be a good church. I used to respect my cousin; he was about three years older than I, but he seemed to be so much more intelligent, and after this, I respected him even more. That day, I gained great respect for that box and felt so proud to know that my church had the Holy Spirit in it.

One day, I was in the woods near the church looking for some firewood for cooking. In those days, we cooked with firewood in an outdoor kitchen built next to the house. In the kitchen, there was a dresser on which the washed dishes were placed, and a fire site, made of wood or stone, where the fire was made for the cooking. So I was in the bushes gathering wood for the fire when I saw my Rector, or Parson, smoking. This worried me, because I felt that a parson is a holy person and should not be smoking.

You see, from a little child I always heard it said it was a wrong thing for a person to smoke, and some even say this was a sin. So I ran home and told my mother what I saw and asked if it was right for the Rector to be smoking. Mother looked at me and, seeing the puzzlement on my face, said, "Yes, my son; it is wrong, but these people don't seem to know better or they just don't care. This is why I don't feel comfortable in this church."

She then went on to tell some of the wrong things this church allowed. For example, each church night, they would end the services on time so those who wanted to go to the movies could go; one of the main members of the church owned the movie theater, and he always left after church and opened up in time so the people could go to the show. Another member owned one of the dance halls, another owned the most popular bar in town, and the church helped them all to prosper. Even though my mother was also enjoying these things and was still a member of this church, I could see that she was not happy. She seemed to have a conscience.

My father always loved to take my mom out, and most times, because I was the eldest of the children, I was the babysitter. Even though it was good for them to spend a lot of time together, and I would gladly encourage all couples to do this, I was a child— what did I know or care? All I knew was that I did not want to be at home alone with my siblings, but what could I do? I was a child, and the child must obey.

Besides me, there were two brothers and one sister. As I said before, there was a time when we never had a TV or radio, and our parents helped to keep us entertained by telling bedtime stores. Many of these stores were about ghost, and because they were good story tellers, the stories had great effect on us. We were afraid of ghosts, so much so that if we could avoid going out at night, we would. Thinking about it now, this was good because it kept us out of trouble. One night, while babysitting my siblings, my sister of about two years old started crying. I did not want her to cry because I was afraid some ghost would hear her and come and take her away, so I hushed her. But she kept on crying; I hit her. She cried even more. I pinched her. Nothing helped. She just cried louder. I became even more afraid, so I pulled the sheet over our heads and lay trembling. After what seems to be an eternity, I heard talking outside. It was Mom and Dad. Thank God! I could now go to sleep. Furthermore, when my Mom and Dad came home, they always brought us goodies: candies, peanuts, and sometimes even ice cream!

We liked this very much. The family lived fairly close together. My grandfather made sure of that. He had his land cut into plots, and each boy child was given a plot of land. The only girl child was not given a plot; she got money instead. The reason for this was explained to me when I was older; if the girl got land on the special property, she might marry and bring some new name to the land. Only Pearts were allowed to build homes on this land.

Life was very good in the evenings after school when our homework was done and we had completed our chores. Most of the kids would gather, girls for baseball and jump-rope, boys for stick-ball, kite flying, marble playing, racing, and such. Sometimes, the adults would come and play with us, but most times they would just stand around and talk. Often, when we really start enjoying our play, we would hear our mothers calling. We never liked it, but no matter how good the games or how happy we were with our friends, when we were called either by mother, father, uncle, aunty, or any other adult, we had to leave what we were doing and go to them or else we would be flogged. This was often done with a stick, belt, or whatever was available at the time.

At times, it seemed like they wanted to kill us, but later we learned that this was for our own good. We learned not to be disobedient, and we were forced to be good to others and our-selves. On the other hand, I have seen children who were allowed to be whatever they wanted to be, act however they wanted to, and most times, get out of control, soon bringing disgrace on themselves and their family. Some even went to jail.

So, the Bible is proven correct when it says in Proverbs 29:15 and 17, "A child left alone to himself brings his mother to shame," and, "Correct thy son, and he shall give you rest," and in Proverbs 23:1, "Discipline may save children from death." In no way am I encouraging abuse to children, but my parents have nine children, and all of us are now serving the Lord; none has ever been to jail, so I do believe that a strict home oftentimes produces good children.

It was Wednesday evening; all the children were now home from school. After we had done our chores and had our dinner, we went outside to play. One of our main play spots was in front of our grandparents' home.

Because our grandparents' home was so close to the main road, sometimes even passersby would stop to watch us play. I think it's because of this up-bringing that even to this day the family still tries to stay together. As soon as we started playing on this Wednesday, Grandma and Grandpa came and took their seats on the veranda, where they could see everything that went on. Today, we were playing ball, and we were allowing the girls to play as well. We picked two teams and a captain for each side, and the game began. Our play went all the way to late evening until it became difficult to see the ball. It was time to end the game, so we said good-bye and everyone went to their own homes.

I do hope by you reading this part of my story that you will see that one thing was very good in this family. No matter what may happen, we always find time to do things together. So many of us get busy with making money and other things, we forget about the family get togethers.

My family was raised to make time for each other so even though we are in a different country, we still find time to get together. I want to encourage this practice. A friend of mine works in a nursing home; she said she feels very sad when she sees some families drop their mothers and fathers off and never return to see them until they have passed away. In some cases, they are buried with no one even showing up. Oh how sad! God bless the family who stick and plays together.

Because we were playing and the place was dusty, we had to wash ourselves before going inside the house. Back in these days, we didn't have pipes with running water in the house, so we did not have a shower; only the rich people had that kind of luxury. Instead, many of the homes had barrels or drums around the house. These drums, as they were mostly called, would contain the water that was so important to our existence. Every family valued this and never wasted it. We got these barrels from the Public Works department of the government. This department was also responsible for the maintenance of the roads. To create and repair the roads, they had to use a material called tar, which came in these big drums. After the drums got empty, you could go to the Public Works and buy them. These drums were then set on the outside of the house with a gutter or lead, a sheet of zinc or any other thing that could be used to direct rain water into the barrel. We depended on rainfall. The water would run off the roof of the house, into the gutter, and into the water-drums. We were very happy for the rainfall and loved when we had a good shower of rain so all the barrels could be filled. If no rain fell, we had to get our pans and go out looking for water. As one of our chores, we would carry the pan with water on our heads back home, and had to make several trips until the drums were filled. When this happened, we could not have our playtime, so we were happy when the rain fell and stopped.

In almost every district, the government ran water pipes. Those who could afford it ran pipes from this into their homes, but for others who could not pay for this, the government would put "stand-pipes" by the roadside. We would then have to take our water pans or buckets, go there, and if water was in the pipe, we would carry the water from there home. Sometimes we would go to one spot and there would be no water in the pipe, so we had to search until we found a pipe with water in it because no one could live without water.

Some homes did not have a pipe with running water but had built-in water tanks. These were big cistern made of stone, sand, and cement that could hold thousands of gallons of water. My grandparent had one of these in their home, and if we couldn't find water any other place this is where we would get our water. Other people would go to the spring, fresh water coming up out of the ground.

No one knows where this comes from, but our great God allowed this so that some people who have no other source of getting water could have water. Sometimes even in dry times, when the rain didn't fall for a long time and most of the water tanks and water pipes had run dry, you could still find water coming from the spring. Isn't God good?

So, for most of the homes, an outside bathroom was built so we could have our bath. We had bath-pans—big metal pans that you could buy at the market. It was big enough for an adult to sit or stand in. We also had tub made of wood and made by a carpenter or a cabinetmaker. This also could be bought from the market. If we wanted a bath, we would take the tub or bath-pan to the bathroom, take water from the drum, pour it into the bath-pan, get in and take our bath. If we needed a shower, we would get in the bath-pan or tub, washed ourselves with soap, and then rinse off by pouring the water all over. It was better when someone poured the water on you; most times the water was cold, but we got used to it. So, because this was done outside, we had to do this before we went inside the house. Sometimes we even took turns bathing each other—girls with girls and boys with boys. This was a much better way to bathe, as another person could reach areas that you may not have been able to reach, and when this was done you felt much cleaner.

So, after washing that evening, we went inside and sat at the dinner table. After having something to eat we went into the living room and sat at the feet of our parents. Noel was about eight years old, Aston was about five years old, and I was about ten. As it was when we were younger, each night before going to bed we sat on the floor and listened to our parents tell stories. We liked this very much and looked forward to such times. Sometimes our parents would not be in the mood, and we would say our prayers and go straight to bed.

Tonight, it seemed as if they did not have time for us; they were talking to each other. We did not interrupt them, because, as I said earlier, we learned not to get into an adult conversation unless we were invited. So we got up and went to sit where we were before, at the dining table. We had not sat down long when Mom called out, "Come here, children." This was not an urgent call, so we knew we were not in trouble. We sat down once more on the floor at their feet.

"Curtis," Mama said. "What would you like to be when you grow up?" This question caught me off guard. Dad did not say anything, but from the look on his face I could see that he also needed to hear my answer. *What would I want to be when I grew up?* I started to think quickly.

I always wanted to be a driver, and as a kid I always boasted that when I grew up I was going to have my own car, so I quickly said, "A mechanic," because every mechanic I knew was always a driver. Then my mother turned to Noel.

"What do you want to be when you grow up?" Without waiting to think, as if the answer was already on his tongue, he said, "A driver."

"Well, Curtis," Mother said. "You are too tender and soft; you can't manage mechanic. Noel is much tougher than you; he will be the mechanic; you will be a tailor." With disappointment in my eyes, I looked at my Dad for support, but he just nodded his head in agreement. I was too soft!

Well, it did not make any sense to protest, because we already knew whatever both of them agreed on, that's the way it was going to be. I later learned that this was a common thing with most working-class and poor families in Jamaica: even though you were still in school, they were not sure how well you would do in school, and they did not want you to suffer in life, so you were encouraged to learn a trade. I saw them talking together, so this must have been what they were talking about. They did not ask Aston any questions. He was still too young. We said good night and went to bed.

The next day started out as other days: we woke up early, took care of the animals (we had goats, pigs, chickens, rabbits, and they all had to be cared for before we left for school). After our chores, we had our breakfast, and off we went to school. We always enjoyed going to school. After school, we had a surprise waiting for us.

While we were in school, mother had wasted no time, and when we got home we found that I had a place where I would learn my trade. My master's name was Mr. Mousy. Mother also found a place for Noel to learn his mechanic trade, and his master's name was Mr. Smith. We would start on Friday. From that day on, every weekend and on holidays we had to go to trade school. After a while we got to love it, because on weekends when we finished we would get some pocket money to go home. We always gave it to Mom, and she would give us spending money out of it.

MY MOTHER GETS CONVERTED

As I said in the last chapter, my parents went out a lot when I was young. One Saturday night, they decided to go to the movies, and I was left to babysit again. So they got us ready for bed and off they went. I lay in bed and listened as they talked outside. The sound of their voices got fainter and fainter until they were gone. I lay on the bed and trembled with fear. I wanted to check the door to make sure it was locked, but I dare not get off the bed because my mind was filled with fear. I never slept a wink until they got home that night. But for some reason, that night was different from all other nights. My mother came home crying, and my dad seemed to be mocking her. I could hear him saying, "Are you a baby? That was only a show," but she kept crying. Nothing he said or did could console her.

The next morning, I learned the reason for her crying. I was now eight years old and understood things a little better. They had gone to the movies and watched a film called *The Ten Commandments*. My mother later told me that when she saw the part with the hand of God writing on the wall and then cutting out the rock, she got converted. Since then, there was something very strange about my mother; suddenly, she looked different.

For example, Mom always had lot of jewelry, and she kept them all in a safe box. I cannot remember seeing her going out without some jewels on her. To my surprise, though, on the morning after her experience at the movies, she took the box of jewels and threw it away. When I asked why she did that, she said she didn't think it was right to be dressed up in so much jewelry because in *The Ten Commandments* the people stripped off their jewels and made an idol with it. Mom was now converted and did not want to do anything to displease the Lord.

As the days wore on, things began getting even stranger. My mother stopped going out on Fridays and Saturdays, even though my father asked her, and on Sunday she got us ready for church, but she stayed home fasting and praying. She told me that she didn't think going to the Anglican Church was going to benefit her new life. My dad could not take this change in my mother and went to his mother for advice.

She advised him to let my mom do what she wanted. He wasn't satisfied with her advice, so he went to his father who told him that, as a man, he was the head of his house and he needed to take command. My grandfather wanted all his family to stay in the family church. He felt that the family always attended this church and they were all fine, so it was the duty of the head of the family to see to it that this continued.

My dad came home and commanded my mother to stay in the family church.

As a child growing up, there was no confusion in calling the Anglican Church the family's church because everyone in the family went to this type of church. Everything that was done in the family religiously was done in this church. Things such as baby christening, marriages, funerals, house blessing, communion, and confirmation. All of the Pearts—great and small, rich and poor—attended this church. As a child sitting at my grandparents' feet, they would tell the story of all the work the family did to help build this great church. This is what helped make this church the family church.

He said, "I'm not going to sit by and allow you to break up our family tradition." This was the cause of many arguments and problems. Every night, I would hear them quarreling; he wanted her to do what he said because this would make him look good to his father and brothers. Because my mom wouldn't obey my father's wishes, he started going out and staying out, sometimes overnight. His constant sleeping out caused even more fights.

I remember one day after my father went to work; my mother fed us then got dressed, packed her "grip" (or suitcase), kissed us, and headed for the door. I asked, "Where are you going?" She said, "I am leaving, and I am not coming back. Your father and I can't get along, so stay inside with your brothers and sisters until your dad come home. I am leaving."

She said this with tears in her eyes, with trembling lips and hands. Even though I was just a small child, I knew my mother was not joking. They had a quarrel the previous night, and now she was leaving before my dad got home. Without any more questions, I fell on my knees and held on to my mom as tight as I could. I prayed for my father to be home. If only he was home! He could help me keep Mom home. Since I had no other help and my kid brother was too small to know what was going on, I did the only thing I could. I held on to one of her feet. She struggled to get free, but I hung on. I knew that I was no match for my mother, but seeing her child down at her feet, crying and holding on for dear life, mother's love made her not shake me off, knowing that she might hurt me.

"Let me go!" she begged, but I hung on even more. "Curtis, let me go! Me and your father can't live together any more. Let me go! I'm leaving! Your father will take care of you and the others."

Finally she stopped fighting to get free, and looking down at me crying and hanging unto her feet, she said, " Okay, I won't go."

"You have to promise me," I said.

"I promise," she said. I did not trust her. I felt that as soon as I let go of her, she would leave. I thought of a way to let her commit to this promise.

"Remember, you say you are a Christian and you can't lie."

"I promise," she said. I finally let go. For the rest of that day and the weeks to come, I kept a close eye on her. I still thought that even though she made me a promise, she might leave when I was not looking. After a while, however, things seemed normal again. My dad finally understood that my mom had changed, so he stopped demanding so much of her; he knew that asking her to change was useless.

WHAT IS BAPTISM?

We continued going to church on Sundays. My mother went along too. We also went to the evening service, but instead of going out after church as she usually did, my mother went home. One morning, my mother told us that she had a dream that she went to a place and there was a preacher baptizing and she went into the water and was baptized too.

"What is baptizing?" I asked. She explained very clearly to me how you go to a pool of water, and they put you down into the water until you are covered. Then they pull you out again. By this way, you are buried under the water. "You can read this in your Bible in Colossians 2:12," she said. Her father was a pastor, and she had been to his baptismal services many times and had seen it being done, so she had no problem explaining it to us. Then, staring off into space, she said, "I want to be baptized."

She went to the pastor of our church the Anglican Church and told him that she wanted to be baptized. The pastor was very understanding; he told her he couldn't do it, but if she knew of a church that was having a baptism, she could go ahead and get baptized because it was the right thing to do. Now that I'm grown and able to look into the Bible for myself, I can see that our Rector was right. According to Matthew 3:13-17, Romans 6:4, Mark 16:16, and Acts 2:38, it was the right thing to do. However, back then, since I belonged to the Anglican Church most of my life, all I knew or learned about was confirmation.

This organization did not believe in baptism; they did things differently. As an infant, you are brought to church with your appointed godparents. Their job was to help watch over and raise you. This was a big day for the family, so most of them attended. The rector, who is like a pastor, took the child to the altar and poured water on its head and prayed over him or her. When you are a teenager, you are then taken back to the rector for confirmation. After speaking with the rector, he agreed with my mother about being baptized but the church did not practice this act and he had to abide by the Anglican church's rules.

According to the dictionary, *confirmation* means to confirm something already done. This means that if you got baptized before, then an act of confirmation can be performed to show the world that some time before, this person was baptized. I remember being confused about this point and asking my uncle, who was an archdeacon, to explain. He said that confirmation is right, because we were baptized into the church as babies and so, when we reached the "age of accountability," we needed to be confirmed. However, I have now been searching the scriptures for some proof of this and found nothing to confirm the Anglican teaching of confirmation.

The Bible *does* talk about blessing babies. In Matthew 19:13-15 and Mark 10:13-16, we see Jesus blessing the children. He laid his hand on them and blessed them. There is no way we could call this event a baptismal service because, as we learn from the Bible and even the dictionary, the word *baptize* means emersion, to be buried or covered.

In Matthew 3: 16, we see Jesus coming up out of the water. You have to be in to get out, right? Acts 8:36-39 recounted a similar story of Philip and the Eunuch. Another point is Jesus waited until He reached manhood before going to the river Jordan and asking John to baptize him. I believe he waited until He knew what he was doing. Furthermore, His mother never had to take Him; He went by Himself. When John tried to forbid him, He said, "Suffer it to be so now for thus it becometh us to fulfill all righteousness." Here, I think Jesus was telling John that you and

I had to be the example for others who will want to know the right way to do this.

Remember, He was supposed to be our light. He said in His Words in the Bible, "I am the light of the world" (John 8:12). Also, in Isaiah 60:1, it says, "Arise, shine for thy light is come." This sounds to me as if we were in darkness; a person in darkness can't really see where he or she is going, but Jesus is our light. He comes shining to show us the way, "and the glory of the Lord is risen upon thee".

Let's look at this example: The sun is the greater light; the moon, the lesser, but it gathers its shining from the sun. When the sun goes down, the moon shines; now everyone can enjoy the moonlight. So Jesus also shines through us and now all the world will see Him through us. Arise and shine, for your light has come! Therefore, I concluded that blessing babies was different than baptizing them, and that baptism was for adults. Because this is such a deep subject, I will deal with this more later in the book.

SEARCHING FOR THE RIGHT CHURCH

Things really changed in our household. Mother had us reading our Bibles at night and praying before going to bed. Early in the morning, we would be woken out of bed to gather in the living room for prayer meetings. I thought this was crazy. Most times we were still sleepy, but we were children and had to obey.

One morning, my mother told us a dream she had that she thought was a warning for us to find a good church in which to worship. In her dream, she was in our yard sweeping up trash when she heard the church bell ringing and saw people going into the church. (This was not shocking because, as I said before, we could look into the churchyard from where we lived.) When she looked up into the sky, she saw the heaven open and the Lord coming, but the people were still going into the church, oblivious to the Lord. She interpreted this to mean that the people of our church were not ready to go to heaven; they were spiritually blind and deaf, and if she continued going there, she too would be lost.

This only made her more determined to find a good church. On the other hand, I was happy with our church. I did not care about another church. My church was pretty with nice pews, good people, and big pipe organs. Moreover, I was about to join the youth choir so I was in no mood to hear such foolishness.

I was about twelve years old, my brother Noel was ten, Aston was seven, and my sister, Veda, was four years old when my mother took us church hunting. After inquiring, we learned that there was another church not too far from where we lived, so we went there for Sunday services. It was so different from the way we worshipped in our church. Here they sang funny, fast songs, and sometimes the people even stood up and clapped their hands as they sang. I had never really seen anything like this before, but I enjoyed it. In my church, it was different. We sang hymns from a book.

The people seemed quite friendly. After church, most of them came to us with greetings and invited my mother back to the evening service. This service was also different from what I was used to. In one part of the service, some people got up and spoke. Later, I learned that this was called testimony. It was the first time I'd seen this. In my church, we sat and the Rector talked. Sometimes, someone may read the scriptures, or they might ask us all to read or say a creed, but this thing of anyone speaking and people standing all over the place giving testimony was strange to me.

I was very surprised when my mother got up and testified. I held my head down, feeling afraid and ashamed, but to my surprise, everyone else seemed happy for her. After that initial visit, we started acting like we belonged to two churches. We attended the new church one week and our old church the next. After a while, I learned that this new church was called Church of God.

My mother also seemed to be falling in love with this new church, but not too long after I found out that she was not too keen on this church because of the lifestyle of some of the members. I remember her saying one day, "I can't leave a hypocritical church to go into the same thing again," so I knew her mind was made up to not abide in this church.

I did not know much about my parents then. We as kids only knew what they wanted us to know, but since my father was gone from home a lot, our bond with our mother grew much stronger, and she talked to us a lot. I also gathered information about them from my cousins from my mother's side of the family who would come to our house and stay with us. From them, I learned about my mother's father, who died before I was born, and found out that he was a leader in a Church of God. From this and other facts, I gathered that my mother was familiar with church life and knew what a "good" church looked and sounded like.

My older cousins coming to spend time with us gave my mother more time to find the church she wanted to attend, and most times, when they were there, she would take me with her. One day, she told me that she heard about a church that was having a baptism and that she was going to be baptized. Even though I used to go almost every place with her, she did not let me attend her baptism.

One day, she came home very excited and told us that she has been baptized. We still belonged to the Anglican church and never really took membership in any other church so, officially, we were Anglican church members and we went there most of the time. This helped our standing in the community and also helped my father to look good. Our father did not come with us on our visits to other churches, neither did he try to stop us, but he never failed to point out that he was opposed to what we were doing.

I, myself, started getting interested in other churches, and the more I visited, the more confused I became. Over time, I found that when I came back to my old church, it seemed as if something was missing. The worship was different; the whole atmosphere seemed different. Eventually, I started looking forward to visiting other churches, and I began to understand how my mother felt. We would walk around the area looking for other churches we could visit. We attended any and all crusades, conventions, and fellowship meetings. We only needed to hear of it and we were there. Still, our spirits had not yet rested on one of these places.

In the meantime, my life was being affected very much. After listening to so many preachers, I found out that I was a sinner, and if I did not repent then I was on my way to hell. I learned that, even though I was a child, I was a sinner and needed to repent and invite Jesus Christ into my life (Romans 3:23, "For all have sinned and come short of the glory God.") The Bible said that the pay I will receive for my sinning is death (Romans 6: 23, "For the wages of sin is death, but the gift of God is eternal life through Jesus Christ our Lord"), but I had hope.

In the word of God, in Romans 10:9 and 1 John 1:9, if we confess our sins, He is faithful and just to forgive us of our sins, and not only forgive us, but will also cleanse us of all unrighteousness. Learning all of this, whenever I heard the Word of God preached and heard the altar call given (that is, someone calling you to the front of the church for prayer), I would rise from my seat or, where there were no seats, push through the crowd to go for prayer, because I really wanted to be saved. I think I may have overdone it.

One of my friends called me "altarpuss," a nickname for someone who kept going to the altar over and over again. But I was young and just coming from an Anglican Church, and these things were happening to me for the first time. I just wanted to make sure that the Lord found me before it was too late. Also, I was confused. When I heard the preacher say to open my heart and let Jesus come in, I did not know how to do that; I was only a child. I knew one thing, though: whatever I had to do to be saved, I must do it. So as a child of about twelve years, I sought for God desperately. At nights I would also hear my mother praying, "Lord, save my children!" She would keep repeating this over and over again, and then she would cry and weep for a long time. This would go on night after night after night.

SATAN BECOME ONE OF MY NEWFOUND FRIENDS

One day, the devil came and paid me a visit. I gave ear to his voice, and we started talking. I was conscious of a still, small voice calling me to turn away from the devil, but Satan's voice was more demanding, so I listened. He told me how wrong my mother and I were to leave our good church and go wondering around the place. I told him how I hated to hear my mother crying almost every day and night. He said she prayed too much. He encouraged me that when I went to school, I should listen to my friends, friends who always tried to get me to do wrong things.

They would tell me that I was too young to be a Christian, and if I became a Christian, I would miss a lot of fun. I tried not to listen, but the truth was that when I was alone, I would think of what they said. Now, the devil was encouraging me to listen to them. After spending some time with the devil, something very strange happened to me. I started hating home; I did not want to hear Mother pray any more in the morning when she woke us up for prayer meetings. I went because I had to, but, kneeling there on the floor, Satan came and joined me, and while the others were praying, he was talking to me. I was a child, but the devil seemed to be very interested in me. He promised to make me great. By the time prayer meeting was over, Satan and I had become good friends. My poor mother! She thought that all her children loved the Lord, but not me; I deceived her, and she never knew.

I started receiving regular visits from my friend Satan. At school, my friends could see that I was changing. They didn't have much trouble convincing me to do the things they wanted me to do. I was becoming popular, gathering friends very fast. I began to hate school, so I started misbehaving. I was thrown out of class and sent to the principal's office on many occasions. I decided not to learn what my teachers were teaching any more. Yes, sir, I would do my own thing.

Then I changed again; I formed a plan in my mind. I became good in school; on the street, I was a model kid. Everyone had only good things to say about me, and when they saw my parents, they would tell them what a good kid I was. I liked this compliment. Sometimes I misbehaved on the street, but if I saw someone I knew coming, I would get out of the crowd and act as if I was not a part of the bad kids. I would also make sure that I was looking neat and fine to meet my mom when I get home.

This was all in my plan. I was going to run away from home and become one of the worst criminals that my country had ever seen. I was going to gather my friends and form a gang. We would live in a cave and gather as many guns as we could find. We would secure our cave by standing guard so no one could catch us unaware. We would go out and steal at night and stay in by day. We would work in the dark so no one would see us until we had everything we needed. Since we were going to be this good, we didn't need education or school, but for the plan to succeed, I must appear to everyone as a very good boy. This way, when I started my crime spree, I would be the last one anyone would suspect.

With my plan all set in my mind, I would still go to prayer when we were called, and after prayer go to bed. While in bed, I could still hear my mother praying and repeating over and over again, "Lord, save my children!" As she prayed, she wept. One night as she prayed, I twisted and turned in my bed. "Oh, God!" I screamed in my mind, "I can't stand this! I can't stand this!" I don't know when I fell asleep, but I know the last thing I heard was my mother crying, "Please, God, save my children!"

Although this used to be also my desire, I did not want to hear this anymore. May I take this time to warn you to be careful of what you set your mind to, or more importantly, how much you allow the devil into your life. He will set you up! Imagine, I allowed the devil to take control and now he was about to set me on the path to destruction. Surely, I know that I would end up dead at an early age.

This is for you parents: don't give up on your children. Keep praying! Even though I wanted my mother to stop praying for me, God only knows what would happen to me if she had. Job 1:5 reads that there was a man name Job in the land of UZ, whose sons and daughters went out partying. Job prayed for them, saying maybe, while partying, they would vex the Lord. This he did continually. You see, Job realized that when his children got together drinking, dancing, and making merry with their friends, they might be tempted to do things to vex God. So even though he was not invited to these young people's party, he took time out to offer sacrifices and prayer unto God for them. Now, may I say this to the youth: one of the reasons why you go out and come in all safe and sound is that most of the time someone is praying for you. Let's be truthful; how often do you remember to pray for the guiding hand of God to take you out and bring you in again?

I HAD A VISIT FROM THE LORD

That same night, I had a dream that my cousin David and I decided to go to my uncle's field to steal some food. While David was busy digging for food, I went to a tangerine tree that was in the field. As I looked up to see if there were any ripe fruits, I saw the face of Jesus looking down on me.

"David!" I called out with a loud voice. "God is watching us!

"Where is He!?" David said.

"Look! Can't you see Him?"

"No!" said he.

"See," I shouted, "He is looking down on us!"

"I don't see any one," he said. I began to run, looking back to see if David was coming, but all I saw was the big face of Jesus watching me. I ran very fast, but I could not outrun Him, and David was nowhere to be found. I just kept on running until I woke up.

In the morning, I told the dream to my mother. She interpreted it for me. She said, "The Lord is seeking after you, and you are running from Him, but you cannot run from God. His eyes are watching you. Listen, my son. God sees and knows everything you do and say." You can't outrun God. From that time on, I feared the Lord even more.

About a week later, I had another dream. I dreamed that my mother sent me to the store to buy bread and sugar. As I climbed the hill to go home, I was able to look straight into heaven. I saw Jesus, and He was busy preparing a great banquet hall. I stood there, watching Him. The tables were all spread with white table clothes with a red cross on them, and He was singing this song:

If you only know the blessing that salvation brings,

You would never stay away.

If you only saw the table spread with lovely things,

You would come to the feast today.

For the door is open wide, and the Savior bids you come.

There is nothing you will have to pay.

So be wise and step inside,

And do not be like those

Who has thrown their only chance away.

His voice was one of the sweetest voices I ever heard! As He sang, He acted as if He didn't know I was there. Then, suddenly, He turned around and said, "Curtis, I have just a few more years to return for My people, and if you wait too long you will miss it."

I told my mother about this second vision, and she just cried. I knew what I had to do; I fell on my face before the Lord and gave my heart to Jesus. That day, He came and dwelt within my heart. I was now about twelve years old.

This should be a warning to young people—Satan is real. He will come and act like he cares about you, but he is only setting you up for death. Don't ever make the mistake I made; Satan hates you because Christ loves you. He wants to see you dead. Read Mark 4:15. Satan's plan is to take God's Words out of you, and He will do this through deception. John 8:44 says, "Satan is the father of lies and there is no truth in him. Sometimes he will even appear like an angel of light."

2 Corinthians 11:14. You see, the devil was once in heaven with God, but he was cast out. Jesus himself said this in Luke 10:18, "I saw Satan like lighting falling from heaven." Because of this, Satan now has a grudge against God, but since he can't hurt God, he is after us.

WE ARE STILL LOOKING FOR A CHURCH

My mother had gotten baptized, I was converted, but we still had not found the church we wanted to settle into. We know that the Anglican Church could not satisfy us; we needed better spiritual food. For many years, my mother had been a member of a top-class church with shiny wood floors, well-polished benches, big pipe organs, and, as a member, an assured burial spot. I had also been there all the while, so we did not want to give up all this before finding something close to what we were leaving. This search only caused more confusion in my mind, so I went to God and prayed, "Dear God, if You are real, please listen to my prayer, and help me, God. I've been going from one church to another, and each one say they are the right church, but I don't know which church is the right one. Please help me, Lord, because I am so confused, and please help my mother to find the place she is looking for. Amen."

One day, a new preacher came to town. His name was Captain Bent. They pitched a tent and had a very big crusade for three weeks. After the crusade, they went into the community center and started having regular services there. Not long after they purchased a piece of land and started building a beautiful church. It was called the Gospel Hall Assembly. He kept meeting in the community center until the church was finished. I thought this was the answer to my prayer, so we started visiting their services, and our visits to the Anglican Church became less and less.

As we kept visiting other churches, it became more evident to my father's side of the family that we were leaving the family church, breaking the family tradition. They began pressuring my father, and he started making problem for us. He became more verbally abusive at home, and he started staying out more. Sometimes, he would stay away for days, and as soon as he got home, there would be fighting. I learned later that, although there were loud quarrels and I could hear things been thrown around, he never hit my mother. His lack of understanding really hurt her, though; he did what he was doing to break her will, but she stood firm.

One day, he ordered us again not to go out to other churches any more, but as soon as the evening came, mother started to get ready for church. There was a crusade going on, and we didn't want to miss it. When I saw this, I got ready too, and away we went to church. Remember, I said before that my cousin came and lived with us, so this made it more easier for Mom and I to go because there was someone trustworthy to watch the smaller kids. We tried to get back before my father got home, but when we tried the door it was locked. He got home before us and locked us out. We could hear him inside saying, "You are not coming in here tonight!" We kept knocking and pleading with him to let us in, but all this seemed to fall on deaf ears. We slept under the cellar that night.

The next day, my father said to me, "You must not follow your mother out to church any more. If you do, I am going to beat you." That night, as my mother got ready for church, I once again got ready too. I was going with her. She reminded me of my father's warning, but how could I allow Mom to go out alone? So I went with her. When we got home, my father let us in this time, but even though mother tried to stop it, I received a good flogging. The next morning, as I sat and inspected the injuries I received from my beating the night before, Mother said, "Keep them to show the angels, my son." These words brought me comfort.

The next week, it happened all over again. My mother and I went to church and were locked out again. This time, we slept outside on a stone. The sleep was very uncomfortable. The next morning Dad got up and went off to work without speaking to us. The next night we went to church again, and we were locked out again. This time, we tried to sleep in the outdoor kitchen, which was also uncomfortable. We were still just visiting other churches; we had not settled into a church.

I HAD ANOTHER VISIT FROM THE LORD

One night, I had a third vision. I dreamed that mother and I went to church, and when we got home we were locked out of the house. This night was different, however, because we heard that the Lord would be passing by, so my mother and I were waiting to see Him. We become separated, though; I could not find my mom, so I climbed a tree to wait for the Lord there. Sometime in the night, the Lord came. He saw me, and we walked and talked together, discussing many things that I could not remember after I woke up.

As we walked, I held unto His left hand. I was so happy walking with Him, and even though this dream is years old, I can still feel the chill running down my spine when I think about it. After a while, He looked down at me standing at his side and said, "Curtis, I have to leave now. I must go back home."

I started to protest. "I'm coming with you, Lord. Don't leave me here."

"No," He said. "You can't go with Me now. Your work on earth is not yet finished. I protested the more, hoping He would change His mind and take me home with Him. I kept holding unto His hand. "I don't want to stay. I do not know which church to attend or who to believe. Everyone says they are the right one. I am confused," I told Him.

He never said another word; He just pointed His right hand. I looked in the direction He pointed, and I saw a man preaching, dressed in a black suite and white shirt. And as he preached, he wiped his face with a white towel he had in his hand. Without another question but still holding onto his hand, I looked up at his face.

He smiled at me and said, "Go, follow that man." I let Him go and stood, watching Him as He went back to heaven. Once again, I told my dream to my mother. The memory of this dream has never left me.

HOW WE FOUND OUR NEW CHURCH

With all we had gone through, I still loved my father, and so did my mom. I remember one night we went out to visit this new church I spoke of, and instead of going the straight way to the church, my mother went another way that took her past the bar where my father usually hung out with his friends. I think she just wanted to see if he was there and if he was okay. She went and looked through the door and saw him there. She seemed satisfied, so we went on our way to church.

As we went on our way, we came upon what seemed to be a building by the side of the road. Someone was trying to build something with some pieces of old zinc, some boards, some canvas, and some wood. We saw that a light was inside, and we heard someone singing. We stopped and examined the structure and peeped through the door. We saw a young man sitting in the front singing, "What a friend we have in Jesus, all our sins and grief to bear."

Inside, there was a lamp hanging from the ceiling with a piece of wire. Later, I learned that this was called a Tilley-lamp. There was a big stone in the center of the building. At closer inspection, it seemed that they were trying to remove it. There were seats made from bamboo. They had driven stakes into the ground and lay the bamboo on top to make seats.

I could see that my mother was becoming interested in this place and seemed to feel sorry for this man who was trying to have church all by himself. I grabbed her hand and pulled at her.

She, knowing that I wanted to go, turned away, and we went on our way. I was glad; my mind was set on going to this new church I spoke of earlier, and I was not about to change this for that old thing I saw there. There was no way I was going to leave my pretty Anglican Church and go to some old canvas junk. What would my friends say? As we went on our way, my mother looked down on me and said, "I am going back."

"What?" I said in surprise.

"I am going back," she said once more. "I feel like attending this little church tonight." But I wanted to go back to this other church, so I began to protest. It was no use; her mind was made up.

We walked into the door of the little church. The man who was singing seemed very happy to see us. He and Mom started talking, and she, pointing to me, said, "This is my son, Curtis." As the man reached out and took my hand to shake it, I looked up into his face. I was shocked to see that this was the same man I saw in my dream, the man who the Lord said to follow! And yes, he was dressed in a black suite and white shirt. It seemed like it was God's will after all. We stayed there and had church, and although we were few, we had a good time. On our way home, we talked about this new church we found, and I had to admit that I did enjoy it.

As I told you before, my mom was a domestic helper and my father was a farmer. One of the homes where my mother worked was the home of Mr. French, the owner of the Pioneer Bus Company. He also owned a guesthouse. Oftentimes my mom would cook for his family and the many guests who stayed in their house. One day, Mom came home and asked my dad if he would be willing to let one of us children go and live with the Frenches.

This was done sometimes in my country when a family gets too big. If both the mother and father agreed, a child would be sent to a friend, a relative, or in this case a rich person who was well known to the family to live with them. They would treat this child as their own. They would send you to school, clothe you, and take care of all your needs. This practice did not mean that the child would be abandoned by his or her family; the child could visit home whenever he wished.

I was now about thirteen years old, and the family had increased. There were now three boys and two girls, so my mother thought it would be fine to send one of us away. My father got angry, however, and said none of his children would leave his house; all his children must grow up together. They argued for a while, and then they agreed that I could go and stay some times but I would not be adopted. Sometimes I wondered what my life would be like if I was adopted.

Anyway, I was allowed to go to Mr. French's home after school, and sometimes when there was no school. This place felt like home to me. There was good food to eat, I could ride the buses for free, and every part of the house was opened to me. I was treated well, and I was happy. Mr. and Mrs. French were strong members of the Anglican Church, so I went to church there more often on Sunday mornings and went to church with my mother at night.

One day, Mrs. French said that she wanted me to join the church youth choir. I told her yes, but I was not sure; I was more interested in my newfound church. We had started visiting this church more often, and before long we fell in love with the pastor and the preaching and teaching. Mother took the right hand of fellowship in this church to become an official member, and we knew that our search was over; we had finally found the place we were comfortable to go to church. We started having a steady growth of people in the church, and many were getting saved. I especially liked it because I was the only young guy in the church and was given special treatment.

Now that we had a church to attend, we went to church more often, and this only increased our trouble at home. Father got more upset, and this seemed affect our relationship with the neighboring family. They were cut off from us, but all this never stopped us. We were present at almost every service, except when I had to attend my other church with the Frenches. It was not long after that, Mom received the baptism of the Holy Spirit and spoke in tongues as the spirit gave utterance as described in Acts 2:1-21. This was also something new to me since we were never taught this in our church.

In Mrs. Jane French's home, some of my chores included washing the dishes and helping to keep the house clean. Sometimes Mr. French would ask me to sweep out and wipe the floor of the buses. He would often come to me and say, "Curtis, if you clean the bus for me, I will give you twenty-five cents." I would clean as much as I could and receive a good reward for my effort. I like this because, of all the kids in my family, I had the most pocket money. When I got home, I would give some money to my other brother and mother and still have money for sport, especially at school.

In those days, the boy with the most money had the most friends at school, so having money made me popular. Even though I had lot of friends, I knew that I was a Christian, and even though some of my friends were bad, I refrained from doing wrong things. I tried to live a life of holiness around them so they too may want to know the Lord for themselves. Yet each day I struggled to keep saved, and my friends constantly showed me how much I was missing because I was a Christian.

I started thinking about what they were saying, and the more I thought, the more it seemed real to me. I was much too young to be a Christian; I would give up and enjoy life now. Then, when I got much older, I would become a Christian again. I did not say this to anyone; I spoke it only to myself in my mind. This is a word of warning to never leave out of the will of God and say one day you will come back to Him. You never know, you may never get the time or chance to come back to God again. Also, please remember that there is nothing hidden from Him; He knows it all. He knows you more than you know yourself. Please remember that no matter what you think in your heart, even though you may not speak it out, God is a heart-reader; there is nothing He doesn't know.

GOD READ
MY MIND

That same night, I went to sleep and had another dream. I dreamed that we were going to one of the villages for open-air service—that is, a service that was held outside of a building. I was carrying the lamp we used for light. (Most places did not have streetlights, so we have to carry our own light.) As we walked along the road, I turned my head and looked back to see if any cars were coming so that I would get out of the way. Nothing was coming. As I looked forward again, I did not see my mother or my pastor. I looked all around and did not see them.

We were just walking together; pastor and my mother were in front, walking and talking, and I was following close behind. Where could they have gone in the short time I took to look back? I looked all around and did not see them. Then, I looked up and there they were, going up in the air. I put the lamp down and cried out, "Mama! Pastor! Wait for me! I am coming." I tried to jump up again and again, but it was as if something was holding me so that I could not rise up to go with them. I jumped and jumped and jumped until I jumped out of my sleep.

I did not tell this dream to anyone, because they would know this was because I was planning to backslide. I just fell on my knees and asked God to forgive me. 1 Thessalonians 4:13-18 has a warning for us that one day, if we are faithful, our Lord will come and take us home to be with Him, and if He comes and finds us not ready, we will be left behind. This is also stated in Matthew 24 and 25. So, if you are one of those who are not serving God, if you have not yet confessed your sins to Jesus and repented and accepted His free salvation plan, then you are heading down a path of destruction.

1 John 1: 9 says, "But if we confess our sins, He is faithful and just to forgive us of our sins and cleanse us from all unrighteousness." You may say you are all right and have nothing to repent of because you have been good all your life, but you still need to repent because "all have sinned and come short of the glory of God" (Romans 3:23).

As you may remember, I spent most of my free time at Mr. French's home. One day, Mrs. French told me that she spoke to my father, and he agreed that I could live there, so I was given my own room. She helped me to fix my room. It had a single bed, so she bought me a cover sheet and a white spread, a pillow with a white pillowcase, and two white lace window curtains for my windows. I could see that she was happy that I was willing to come and live in her home, as all her children were grown and had left home. So even before I decided to live there, I was treated as their own child. After bringing me all these things for my room, she helped me fix my room. When it was finished, it looked so good; I was so proud of my room that I even called some friends to see it.

After a while, I started missing my home and family, and this caused me to feel homesick. I was not going to church as much as I wanted to, and this made me long for church. I finally told Mrs. French that I wanted to go home. She got so upset. She argued with me for a while, but when she saw that my mind was made up and that I wanted to go home, she started crying and ran to find her husband. After they spoke, they decided to let me go. When they did, I suddenly had mixed feelings; I felt like I was ungrateful. After they had done so much for me, I wanted to go home. Yet I was happy to go. I was away from my home, my family, for three weeks, and I missed all of this. I wanted to go home. Mrs. French pointed out to me that I was making a big mistake and said that she was not going to touch my room because she believed I would be back. They spoke to my parents and sent me home. I learned a big lesson: No matter how poor your home seems to be, there is no place like home.

When I arrived home, I was received by everyone as a lost child returning home. My sisters and brothers gathered around me with lots of hugs and kisses. Yes, it was so good to be home. I never really stop visiting Mrs. French, and even though she was angry with me for leaving her house and returning home, in a little while everything was back to normal.

Now that I was back home, I was able to visit church more often. I fully surrendered my life to the Lord, and I sought more and more to please Him. I was a very good singer, and the people who visited the church said they could hear my voice even when they were far way from church.

THE NEW ME

At the age of eleven years old, I went to my pastor and told him that I was now ready to be baptized, but he refused and told me to wait some more. I think it may have been that he saw me as a child who didn't really know what I was doing. Anyway, above everything in church, I loved to hear my pastor teach. I never missed a time of teaching, and his teaching helped me to grow strong in the Lord.

One of my favorite things to do was to go into the bushes and pray. I would find a place to pray while in school during a break, instead of going out to play. I would go to pray on a hill with great big rocks and lot of trees behind the schoolhouse. It was a great place to pray, and every day I would find some time to spend with my Lord. So you see, it is very easy to live for Christ wherever you are. Oftentimes I hear Christian youths say that it's too hard to live for God while in school, but once your mind is made up to be holy, you will live for Christ any place and any time, no matter the circumstances.

We are living in a polluted world, but you don't have to be polluted. Look at the fish; even though they live in the salty sea, when you catch them and cook them, if you do not add salt to them, they will have no flavor. You have to add salt because they are fresh; even though they live in the salty sea, They are not contaminated by their surroundings. Therefore, As a Christian, you also can live in this sinful world and not be contaminated by it. It's not you that live, but it's the Christ that lives in you and me. Yes, we can make it!

Remember David; he was not afraid to face Goliath, even though Goliath was a man of war and had experienced many wars. He was big, mighty, and strong, but David, just a youth, knew that his God was bigger, mightier, and stronger. When he faced Goliath, he said to him, "I come to you in the name of the Lord my God" (1 Samuel 17).

Also, remember Joseph who, when forced by his master's wife to commit adultery, refused and ran from her. He said these words to her as he left his coat in her hands and fled, "How can I do this wicked act and sin against my God?" (Genesis 39). Look at the three Hebrew boys who, against great odds, refused to bow and worship the king or his golden image and were cast into the fire (Daniel 3). Here, we learn how God is a present help in time of trouble.

My young ones, remember what our brother Solomon said in Ecclesiastes 12, "Remember now thy creator in the days of thy youth." Now is the time to seek the Lord. Pray this prayer with me:

"Dear Lord, I am Your child who has wandered away from You. I am sorry, Lord. Right now, I repent of my wrong. Please forgive me and make me Your child again. Thank You, Lord."

Most of my young days were spent with the Lord. I feared God, and He loved me. I can remember one day at a school picnic, what was known in those days as a fair. All the children looked forward to this day. This was a time set apart to have fun. This was a time when everyone would get together and forget about school, forget about work; all schools were closed and all work stopped. Mothers and fathers from everywhere would be there with their children. There was a lot of food and ice cream and a lot of merry-making. Most of my friends were going to be at this year's fair. I put on some of my best clothes, and so did my brothers and sisters; we all got ready, and off we went to my old school grounds where the picnic was being held. We did not live far from this place, so we almost ran all the way.

When we got there, I was surprised to see some of my friends and relatives were already there. I wasted no time; I quickly joined in the fun, but something was wrong. This was something we did every year, but this time I could not seem to enjoy myself. I took a walk to the merry-go-round, gave the attendant two pennies, and took my seat. *Oh yes; this is fun, round and round we go.* "Hold on tight!" the men shouted as we went round and round. *Yes, this is fun. I am finally enjoying myself.* After going around for about ten times, we came to a stop.

"Everybody off!" the attendant shouted. I hopped off and walked over to the ice-cream man. I bought a cone and then went over to the maypole—a bamboo pole planted in the ground with lot of different colored ribbons hanging from the top. Some men and woman held onto the ribbons. The man we called "Shorty" was there playing the fife, while other men played on the drums. It was good music, and as it played, the men and women holding the ribbons danced around the pole, each going in the opposite direction. When the music stopped, all the ribbons were braided together in a pretty pattern, and all the children looked on in amazement. Then the music started again, and the dancers danced in reverse until all the ribbons were untangled again. At the end, these dancers rested, and another set of dancers started the dance all over again.

At the end of the dance, I went to find my brothers and sisters. It never took long for me to find them. I then went to my grandmother, who was selling drops and grater-cake (cakes made with coconut and sugar) in a special spot at the school gate.

Since I mentioned my grandmother, I want to pause here to talk about her. She was my father's mother, the only grandmother I can remember. (My mother's mother died when I was very young, so I did not know her.) She was loving and treated all her grandkids as if we were her very own children.

I remember one day I went to see her. I especially loved to visit her when she was making sugar cakes, because she would give me the "duchy" (the pot in which she made the cakes) to wash, and, as you may surmise, she always left some sugar in the bottom. This day that I went to visit, I saw my grandmother in a state I will never forget. My granny, who was always a happy, merry woman, was crying. This was the first time I ever saw her sad. Tears were flowing down her ruddy face. I tried to find what went wrong with her. She said, "Oh, my child," and murmured under her breath something about a lie. I took that to mean that someone had told a lie on her, and she did not want to talk about it, at least not to me, a child. She continued crying, singing, "Must Jesus bear the cross alone and all the world go free? No, there is a cross for everyone and there is a cross for me."

As the tears streamed down her face, she finished that song and began to sing, "What a friend we have in Jesus, all our sins and grief to bare; what a privilege to carry everything to God in prayer." Then she stopped singing and started praying, "Father, please forgive them." Then she continued singing. Even though I was just a child, this picture of my grandma never left my mind.

So that day at the fair, I spent some time with my grandmother at the school gate, eating some sugar cakes before going back to enjoy the fair. I met up with a few of my friends, and together we started touring the place. We visited some game spots, laughed and played a bit, and then we decided to go into the dance hall. As we walked inside, I saw that the rector was there too. He seemed to be enjoying the fun so surely this couldn't be bad. We all knew that the rector was a holy man of God and if this was a bad place to be, then he would not be here.

I went in. All my friends were dancing. My godfather was there, and so were some of my uncles and aunties and many others I knew. They all seemed to be having a good time. I joined the crowd and began to dance. Suddenly, a thought flashed in my mind: Suppose while I am dancing the Lord should come. I knew that I would be lost, so I moved out of the crowded area and went by a window. As I danced, I kept looking up into the sky, because I said if God should come while I am inside the dance hall, I would see and run out of the dance and get to go with the Lord.

As I kept thinking of this, I realized that I was not enjoying myself, so I said good-bye to my friends and went out of the dance hall. I felt relieved to be outside. Surely, it's true—children of God must be mindful of the places they go. There was a song that we often sang in our church that said "places I used to go, I go there no more; things I used to do, I do them no more; words I used to speak, I speak them no more. It's a great change since I was born; it's a great change since I was born."

The place where this picnic was being held was the same school I attended. I had a special spot to pray among the rocks, so this day, with all the fun around me, I once again found my way to this place of prayer, and there I spent some time with the Lord. After praying for some time, I went back to my grandmother and stayed there until it was time to go home. I know that you may be thinking that this was weird, but you must remember I was just a young child who, since I come to know the Lord and found out that there is heaven for me to gain, feared that if I was not careful I might miss heaven, and there was nothing I wanted more than to be in heaven when my time in this world is over. The picnic went on until late evening. I shared my experience with my mother, and she was happy that with all the fun, I had time to seek the Lord.

WHAT ABOUT BAPTISM?

Remember that at the age of eleven, I had asked my pastor to baptize me and he refused, asking me to wait some more. Well, to be honest, I was a bit disappointed because I knew I was saved and was determined to go on with my Lord. May this be a lesson to those who may be looking at the size or age of someone.

Almost everywhere I went and stayed for a while, I would always find a place to make an altar before my God. I spent many hours of my days in some rocky places, among the trees, in many valleys before the Lord. So while I was been judged from the outside, I was doing my best to live holy before the Lord (like Abram in Genesis 17:1, when God said to him, "Walk before me and be thou perfect," or David and his brothers in 1 Samuel 16:5-13).

It was September 1967, and we were having convention. It was a good convention; many souls came to know the Lord as their personal savior. Usually after a convention when people came to know the Lord, the next step would be baptism, so in the weeks that followed the new converts went through counseling and then baptism was planned. So once again, I asked my pastor if I could be baptized. My pastor asked my mother, and she agreed and talked it over with my father. I was allowed to attend preparation class. I could not believe my dad agreed to allow me to be baptized; he must have been changing. Baptism was set for the last Sunday in the month of October 1964. There was not much time, so we had teaching and counseling in preparation for our baptism day.

You may be wondering why I was making so much fuss about baptism. You see, growing up in the Anglican Church, we all had a misunderstanding of baptism, how it was to be done, and what was the significance of it. As far as I was told, I was baptized as a baby, but I have no such memory of this because I was only a child. Here are some questions we needed to look into: First, what does a baby know about sin? Second, can a baby confess his or her sins (as Matthew 3:1-6 said we should do)? Third, can a baby be sorry for committing sins and ask for forgiveness (1 John 1: 9), as we all need to do to receive salvation?

We must acknowledge that we are sinners, we must be sorry for our sins, we must confess—not necessarily to man, but to God—and repent to be saved. A person is not saved by attending church, paying your tithes or offerings, or by being good. These are works, and no one can be saved by works. These are what you do after you are saved. Then, you need to be baptized. Please note that baptism does not save you; you must be saved then be baptized as a sign to the world that you have put off the old self and put on the new man, Christ Jesus.

I had given my life to God, so now I needed to be baptized. Take an example from Jesus. As a baby, His parents took Him to the temple. He was just eight days old, a baby. They took Him to present Him to the Lord. There, a man named Simeon took the child Jesus in his arms and blessed Him (Luke 2:21-32). Later, however, we see Jesus, when He was about thirty years old, walking to the river Jordan to be baptized by John (Matthew 3:13-17). Would you not say this is a good example?

Let's see if we can answer this question: What is baptism? Most of our dictionaries have many different answers for this question, but since we all want to be sure that we are doing the right thing, it's only right that we take time and investigate this topic. To be fair, I will hold back what I believe until we research this together.

Just as a library is a place where there are many books, even so, your Bible contains many books. Now, when you are doing research, you need to look into materials that are trustworthy and also talk to people who are trustworthy. Your Bible fully qualifies on all these points and more. You see, your Bible has withstood the test of time and has received the approval stamp by God Himself. In fact, it is the word of the Almighty God in written form, so now let's take this precious library and get to work.

Two of the most frequent forms of baptism practiced by most of our churches today are sprinkling and immersion. I Peter 1:2 deals with the sprinkling of the blood of Jesus upon the altar of our hearts, an act that refers to hearing the gospel and receiving salvation. Isaiah 52:15 also spoke of sprinkling, but this is not water baptism as some think, but rather the spreading of the gospel to the nations after the death of Jesus Christ. This was a prophesy and should not be interpreted incorrectly.

It will surprise many to know that it refers to the fast way the word will spread, and many, after trying to stop it, will have to shut their mouths because what they don't hear they will see, and what they don't hear they will consider. What we need to do is allow the blood of Jesus to reach our hearts. I don't think scriptures that speak about sprinkling with water—such as Ezekiel 36:25, Hebrews 19, and Numbers 8:7—are saying we must sprinkle with water as a form of baptizing. Did you find other scriptures that talk about sprinkling, for there are a lot of them in the Bible. Did any of them encourage us to baptize our babies? So why do we do it when God did not tell us to?

Now, baptism by immersion was a new thing to me. It may seem that I am contradicting myself; I am writing that I don't believe in babies being baptized, but here I am, a baby, in your eyes, seeking to be baptized. Well, I do not consider a child of eight years old a baby. There is nothing in the Bible that said a child can or should not be baptized. I believe that as long as you are old enough to understand that doing wrong is sinning, you should repent and seek the Lord. Then, I believe that you can be saved, and, after being saved, you must be baptized.

You may ask why, then, did Jesus wait until the age of thirty years old before He was baptized. I think this was to remove all confusion from us as to who should be baptized and when. He made sure to wait until He reached manhood before He asked John to baptize Him.

Now, let's look at baptism by immersion. Before I started attending the Church of God, all I knew was baptism by sprinkling. I am only a child, and I am not afraid to confess that I didn't know everything. Anyway, since I began attending the Church of God, I learned a lot. So, what is baptism by immersion? The word *immersion* means to be covered, hidden from sight. Another meaning is to be put under or go under, to be buried.

Now, let's take a look at some scriptures. Before we do so, what's the use of baptism? This ordinance is a symbol of the Christian's identification with Christ's death, burial, and resurrection (Romans 6:4, Colossians 2:12, and Acts 8:36-39). In other words, it's a testimony to the world that there is a change; the Lord has found you, and there is a great change. This is why I wanted to get baptized all those years.

Back then, I wanted to be very sure I was doing the right thing in this Christian walk, so I read Romans 6. This is a very good scripture to read for this subject, but let's look at verse four, which says, "Therefore, we are buried with Him by baptism into death that, like as Christ was raised up from the dead by the glory of the Father, even so we should walk in the newness of life." What is this really saying?

It's saying now that we have turned our life over to Christ, so we are spiritually dead to sin and sinful things of this world. If we are dead, then we must be buried with Him. Now, He is not asking us to dig a grave in the ground and ask someone to bury us, but He is referring to baptism in water, as Colossians 2:12-14 explains. Also, according to 1 Corinthians 15, when a believer goes through the ceremony of baptism, he or she is made to identify with the death, burial, and resurrection of our Lord and Savior Jesus Christ. Now, let's look at the baptism of our Master Teacher as discussed in Matthew 3. Jesus was holy; He did not have to be baptized because He was God. Also, in a few months, His death, burial, and resurrection would happen to Him for real, but let's take a walk down to the river Jordan.

There was a strange man who lived in the wilderness of Judah named John. He ate locusts and wild honey for his meal; He also dressed very weird: His raiment is camel's hair and a leather belt around his loins. And he was preaching a strange message. He was saying, "Repent ye for the kingdom of heaven is at hand; make your path straight."

As he preached, many people came out of Jerusalem, Judea, and the entire region around Jordan, and he was baptizing in Jordan those who were willing to confess their sins. As he baptized, he saw some people attending his baptism. He perceived that they were not saved, and they were not there to be saved; they just came to spy, find fault, and make trouble; they were not even there to seek repentance. He turned to them and said, "Oh generation of vipers! I warn you: Flee from the wrath to come. Repent of your sins, and bring forth fruits that show that you are converted. If you don't, I tell you this, the ax is now laid at the root of the trees. Soon you will be cut down and cast into the fire."

Then, he turned to the people and said, "I indeed baptize you with water, but there is coming one after me. He is much greater than I; His shoes I am not worthy to bear. He shall baptize you with the Holy Ghost and with fire." Then John turned his gaze to a young man coming toward him. It was Jesus. Everyone's eyes turned to this young man. What was He doing here? Did He come to baptize John?

He stepped into the water; He is either going to baptize John or some of the other people with John. Look! He is stepping into the water! Yes, I think he is going to baptize John or maybe baptize some of the people for John. John was saying that this young man was mightier than he, so maybe He was coming to baptize him. As Jesus spoke to John, the crown drew near and one of the young men asked John to baptize him too. "Look!" Now He's talking to John. "Let's draw near." The young man is asking John to baptize Him, but John refused Him saying, "I have need to be baptized of You and Thou comest to me?" But Jesus answered him, saying, "Suffer it to be so now for thus it becometh us to fulfill all righteousness."

Then John baptized Him. Jesus, when He was baptized, went up straightway out of the water. Now pay attention to these words: *He went up straightway out of the water.* He had to be down to come up and in to come out. The Bible also said, "Out of the water and lo the heavens were opened unto Him and He saw the Spirit of God descending like a dove and lighting upon Him and lo a voice from heaven saying, 'This is My beloved Son in whom I am well pleased." Oh, glory to God! This makes me want to run around the house with my hands in the air and worship! You can see by this that Jesus did His baptism as an example to us. Also, He went down in the water and came up, marking His death, burial, and resurrection.

This is expected of all true believers; once you accept Christ in your life, you must follow His example. Let's look at another story; I enjoy true stories. Acts 8:26-40 speaks of a man of God named Phillip. One day, the angel of the Lord spoke to him and told him to go south, the way that lead from Jerusalem to Gaza. Even though the place was a desert, Phillip obeyed. He looked and saw a chariot coming. On the chariot was a man from Ethiopia, a man of great authority. As Phillip watched, the man approached him, and the Spirit said, "Go join thyself to the chariot."

Philip walked up to the chariot and asked the man if he could join him. When the man said yes, Phillip climbed aboard the chariot. He found that the man was reading a book of the Bible.

(Remember, we cannot say he was reading the Bible, because in those days the Bible was not yet available. The Bible is a book of many books, and it was not yet compiled when Philip met the Ethiopian. Each book was separate and known as scrolls or parchments folded together.) So, Phillip found this man reading from the book of Isaiah. Philip also learned that the man went to Jerusalem to worship and was now on his way home. Phillip asked of him, "Understandeth what thou readeth?" The Ethiopian answered, "How can I unless someone explain it to me?" Oh, how powerful is our God! He saw that this man needed to understand His words, and so He sent Philip right in time to him. Blessed be the Lord!

The scripture he was reading from was the book of Isaiah, which said, "He was led as a sheep to the slaughter and like a lamb, dumb before his shearer, so he opened not his mouth" (53:7-8). Matthew 26:62-63 says that as Phillip explained this scripture to the man, they came to a body of water. The traveler said to Phillip, "See, here is water. What doth hinder me to be baptized?" Phillip said, "If thou believest with all thine heart, thou mayest," and he answered, "I believe that Jesus Christ is the son of God." The traveler then commanded the chariot to stand still, and they both went down into the water. Note these words again: down into the water. Phillip baptized him, and when they were come up the Spirit of the Lord took away Phillip so that the Ethiopian saw him no more, and he went home rejoicing.

MY BAPTISM DAY

I knew I was saved and needed to be baptized. The baptismal service was to be held in a different village. My home church was in Christiana, Manchester, but my church was going to join with another church in the parish of Trelawny, in the village of Wait-a-bit. There were seven people from my church being baptized, and, as you may guess by now, I was the youngest. The church in Wait-A-Bit had five candidates, so this was set out to be a big baptism.

I was looking forward to my baptism; I had waited a long time for this. Some people from that area went to the river, cleaned out a spot, and built a dam in the river to push more water into the spot so that there would be a hole deep enough to have the baptism. You see, to have an easy baptism and to make it easy for the pastor to dip us, the water had to be at least up to our waist.

The baptism would be early morning, so, since Wait-A-Bit was far from Christiana, Pastor made arrangements for us to spend the night with members of the church there. The rain fell all night. Early the next morning, everyone gathered at the church for final instructions, singing, some testimonies, and prayer.

While this was going on, one deacon and two brothers of the church went to the river to make sure all was well for the baptism and sent back bad news to the church. The pastor of that church made an announcement. He said that because of the rain last night, the river "came down" and washed away the spot that was prepared for the baptism. Furthermore, even though the river was becoming calm, it was still rough and a little dangerous to get into.

I know that there are some of you readers who are wondering what I am talking about, much less to see one "coming down." For some of you, the rivers you know are so big that, unless you pay close attention, you wouldn't even know that the river is "coming down." By "coming down" I mean it rose above its usual level. In Jamaica, when the river "came down," it overflowed its banks, flooded the land, and sometimes it destroyed anything in its path—trees, animals, farms, and homes.

Because of the force of the river, nothing stood a chance in its path. When the rain falls heavily, water comes down from the hillside and flows into the little streams. These streams then flow into the river, and the river collects much more water than it is used to.

This river that we love to play in becomes a mighty force to contend with. When the river is calm, the water is clean and pretty as it flows over and around the river stones. On a hot day, nothing feels better then jumping in to cool off. Sometimes, we would swim or fish in the river, and sometimes we would even drink from it. But when the river "comes down," you cannot do any of those things; the water is dirty and muddy and rough—it is best to stay away.

There were two pastors and some deacons and church members had to make a decision; should they postpone the baptism, or should the baptism go on? After talking together, they decided the baptism should go on.

Whenever there was a baptism, there was always a parade from the church to the place of baptism. We all gathered in a long line, walking in threes and fours, depending on the wideness of the road. (Sometimes, we had to travel along the main road, and vehicles had to pass.) Sometimes, when the crowd got too big, we had to get help from the police. This is how we lined up, police in front, on the side, and behind the crowd. Their job was to make sure all went well.

The officers were in the back and in the front were the ministers, followed by the music—because there was singing and dancing all the way—then the candidates who were going to be baptized Behind the candidates ladies in white and men in black-and-white, then the crowd, singing and dancing. As we went on, the crowd would get bigger, because as the parade passed the homes, people would leave their homes and join the march.

On that morning when we came to the place of baptism, the river was still rough, but it was not too bad. Some men went into the water and prepared a spot for the baptism. In the meantime, the service continued on the bank of the river. Those who were going to be baptized stepped forward and testified before the crowd. These testimonies were usually about how the Lord saved and kept us and how we have made up our minds to keep living for Him.

After this, deacons entered the water, followed by the minister who was going to perform the baptism. When he confirmed that all was safe, he called for the first candidates. (In these services, especially for the ladies, if the ground was unstable, two deacons would take you to the water's edge, one on either side. The two deacons in the water would take you to the minister to be baptized.)

One at a time, the minister told the candidates to lift their right hands and repeat these words: Thy vows are upon me, oh Lord, until death. We were asked to say this three times, after which he, with the assistance of a deacon, held each of us with a firm hand and said, "Upon the confession of your faith and the word of your testimony, I now baptize you in the name of the Father, the Son and the Holy Ghost. Amen." He then dipped us in the water, making sure we were fully covered.

I will never forget this experience. Even now, after thirty-nine years, I can still remember it as if it were yesterday; I can still see myself in the water—its dirty color—and feel the coldness and hear the voice of the pastor telling me what to say; I can still feel myself being pushed down under the water and remember being afraid of being swept away by the water, gaining confidence when I felt the strong hands of the pastor and deacon holding me. On the contrary, I cannot remember anything of my "baptism" as a baby in my old church.

One day, after my baptism, I asked my pastor why he was so intent on making sure I went under the water. He explained that, according to the Bible, I am spiritually dead, and when you are dead, you have to be buried. He said that if a person is dead and you take some dirt and sprinkle on them, after a few days no one could stay around the place because of the stink it would cause. So it was in the Lord; we were now dead, so we must be buried.

After my baptism, I was very interested in the Lord. My pastor was a very good teacher and, apart from Sunday school, at least one day of each week was set apart for teaching the Bible. I loved to be in Bible studies and never missed a night. I kept taking in more and more of the word. I also found that the closer I got to the Lord, the sweeter He became to me. The Bible says, "Draw nigh to God and He will draw near to you" (James 4:8). So it was becoming very common for me to go into the bushes, sometimes to pray, sometimes to gather wood for the fire, and, even if I went to gather wood for the fire, I would often sing and pray while doing so.

One day while in the woods among the rocks, I heard someone calling me. When I tried to see who it was, I found no one. This happened a few times before I finally understood that this may be the Lord calling me. So one day, I went to my favorite spot and prayed, "Dear Lord, I do not know You like I am supposed to, but I desire so much to know You and find Your will for my life. Whatever You want of me, do it in me, oh Lord. Amen." As I finished praying and walked away, I was assured that the Lord heard my prayer. I could feel the presence of the Holy Spirit around me. There was a sweet sense of joy, peace, and happiness all around me. I went on my way rejoicing.

I had always said that when I grew up, I wanted to be a doctor. One thing I never thought of becoming was a preacher. I can't really say why, but I found, in most of my family, when we speak we don't speak clearly enough to be easily understood. This I found mostly from my father's side of family. I also seemed to have this problem: When I spoke, my speech was never very clear, and this was embarrassing.

Sometimes when I stood up in church and tried to testify, I saw the young people laughing at me as I struggled to get my words out. You could see the compassion on the faces of the people in my church; they seemed to feel sorry for me. Because of this, I knew that I would never be a preacher, because in my thinking you had to be a good speaker to be a preacher. Still, my speech didn't stop me from speaking in my church. In most Church of God churches, in night services they would have what is called a testimony service, where the saints would gladly stand up and tell of the goodness of the Lord. I would always stand up to share what He had done in my life too.

I must have been judging everyone wrongly; imagine my surprise when, at about the age of sixteen, my pastor started allowing me to go up in front of the congregation and bring a word. This become more frequent over time, and, even though the church was now filled with people—a lot of them as young as I was or older—my pastor would place much focus on me. Before long, he had me preaching on the street in open-air meetings.

I can still remember my first message, taken from Revelation 22:12. My topic was "Behold, I Come Quickly." I was on the street side in a place called Sedburge under a shop front. The anointing came down on me, and I *did* preach. After this, preaching became the norm for me. I was also a good singer and would often represent the church in their concerts and rallies at other churches. With all this happening in my life, I became bold and was doing something for the Lord every opportunity I got.

As young people in the church, we also had good times. We had no need for what the world had to offer because we would have fun playing Christian games together. We sometimes visited each other's homes. There would be no fighting, cursing, or swearing; our church sisters were happy around us because of our Christian attitude, and even if we had it in our minds to go out of the way, we would not because it might get back to our church and we would be in trouble. So, at all times we were on our best behavior.

BE FILLED WITH THE SPIRIT

I had no idea what being filled with the spirit meant. I never knew how to go about asking the Holy Spirit to come and live in me. I never even knew that this was in the Bible. After reading it in the word of God and hearing my pastor and others teach and speak on this, I understood that this was a provision made by God for His children. He wanted to live in us. Look to these scriptures in John14:16. Jesus said, "And I will ask My Father and He will send you another comforter and He will abide with you forever." Verse seventeen says, "Even the Spirit of Truth who the world cannot receive because it seeth Him not, neither knoweth Him. But ye know Him; for He dwelleth with you and shall be in you."

Jesus' time on earth was now coming to an end. When His followers learned this, they got worried. Jesus was a real comfort to them; when they were sick, He was their healer; when they were hungry, He gave them food; when they were troubled in any way, He solved their problems. He was telling them He had to go.

Followers knew that Jesus was their promised Messiah and, according to what they had learned from the prophets, when the Messiah came He would restore to them the kingdom. In their minds, they were just waiting for the time when He would take back the kingdom from the Romans who were tormenting the Jews. After building up much hope in this man, He was now talking about leaving.

Like so many today, could not differentiate between an earthly kingdom and a heavenly one. Jesus said to Pilate in John 18:36

that His kingdom was not of this world. Jesus told His troubled disciples that when He got home, the Father would send them another comforter to be with them forever. This last phrase is very important and is saying the comforter will live in us.

Look at this promise in Joel 2:28-32. You should take some time to read this, as it was a prophecy, given even before Jesus came on the scene, that in the last days God would "pour out of His Spirit upon all flesh, and your sons and daughters will prophesy, your old men will dream dreams, and your young men will see visions, and also on My menservants and My maidservant I will pour out of My Spirit." This was referring to everyone. Now don't believe that because I said everyone I meant the ungodly as well; God will never put His Spirit in an unclean vessel. Notice the phrase said "My menservants and My maidservants." This means those that are His. So the Holy Spirit just doesn't come upon us. He wants to indwell us. Look at 1 Corinthians 3:16-17, 1Corinthians 6:19-20, Luke 1:15, John 14:26, Acts 8:15-16, Acts 4:8, Acts 4:31, and Act 2:4. These are just some scriptures that prove that God wants us to receive the Holy Ghost.

From then on, I sought for the infilling of the Holy Ghost. I had a great craving for the Holy Ghost; I sought Him every chance I got. I needed Him so much. I felt incomplete without Him in my life, so every place I went I was always seeking for an opportunity to have this infilling of the Holy Ghost.

My home church was in Christiana, Manchester, but we had some satellite churches. One such one was located at Sedburge district. We had a convention there that went on for one whole week. One day in this convention, after kneeling at the altar and praying for a while, I was led away in the spirit into a new realm where I had never been before.

When I came to myself, I was speaking in another tongue. By this I mean that I was speaking in a new language I did not understand (as seen in Acts 2:3), but as soon as I knew this was happening, I stopped it. You see, I was always afraid of being false; I did not want to be a false prophet. As far as I was concerned, false prophets say and do things in the name of God, but are not led by God; they are an abomination unto the Lord, and I surely wouldn't want to be that.

After that day I never spoke in tongues again, until about six month later when I was in church and my pastor asked us to prepare for prayer. Sitting on the second row, I bowed my head to pray, when suddenly it come pouring out. First, I didn't know what was happening. Then, when I finally came to and saw what was happening, I just gave up and let the Spirit have his way. I was consumed with a joy. My body humbled itself to the Holy Ghost, and I was edified in a way that I have never been since. I had given my heart to the Lord. This experience proved to me that the Lord is real and that there are higher heights and deeper depths in the Lord.

Have you received the Holy Ghost since you became saved? If not, just ask Him in and surrender yourself to Him, and He will come in. Some people have given up seeking for the filling of the Holy Ghost because they have been listening to so much junk and some even allow false doctrine to enter their minds. Here is what some people believe: as soon as we become a Christian we are Holy Ghost filled. I have learned differently. There is "*with* you and an *in* you."

The Bible teaches us clearly that the child of God experiences God's power by blood, water, and fire. To explain further, when you come to Jesus confessing your sins and accepting salvation, you are saved through the blood. You then go to your pastor, who proceeds to baptize you in water. After this baptism you must now invite the Holy Spirit to live in your heart. The spirit will come and fill you; once this occurs, you are now spirit filled. Joel 2:28-29 speaks about this filling, also Act 1:4-5, 8:17-18, Luke 11:24, and John 14:16.

There are so many Holy Ghost-filled Christians in this world. Do you think all of these people are wrong? Well, I am a witness in this case; God is real and He wants to live in you. Won't you let Him in today? You will find Him to be a real friend.

THE TWO- AND SIX-PENCE BLESSING

There are many people living among us who do not believe in the existence of a true, living God. In the following chapters, I will tell you some true stories, and you can decide for yourself if God is real. I will begin with a story that my mother told me about when we were experiencing some difficult times.

"There was nothing to feed my children," she said. "Soon they will be coming home from school. I searched through every drawer, on every tabletop, on the shelves, hoping that maybe I might find some money; anything I found would be a blessing. Six pence could buy a pound of cornmeal, and with this I could use to make a meal for everyone. But after searching every place there was nothing. Since I did not know what else to do, I stood in the center of the house and prayed, 'Oh Father, my Father, there is no food in the house. My children will be home soon from school, and there is nothing to feed them with. You, Lord, said when I am faced with problems like this, I should ask, so here I am, Lord, asking of You. Help me, Lord.'

"Just then, I heard a voice say, 'Go to your room.' When I did, the voice said again, 'look on the chest.' I did, and I could not believe my eyes. Right there, in plain view, was a two- and six-pence piece. Right in my eyesight!"

Let me pause here to explain what a two- and six-pence piece is. Many years ago, Jamaica was under the rule of England, and so the currency money we used was the pound, shilling, and pence. A two and six pence piece was one silver coin with that name.

"This was an answer to prayer," my mother said. "Almost every day, I cleaned and dusted this place, so how could this get there? This was the doing of the Lord." She lifted it up to heaven and thanked the Lord for such a precious gift. This was enough money to have a very good dinner. My friends, from this story, is God real or what?

HOW GOD PROVIDED MY SHOES FOR SCHOOL

I was now fourteen years old. All the children in my class and of my age had now outgrown the primary school. We would be sent to the Christiana Secondary School. This was a different life setting for me. You see, while I was attending the primary school, many children whose parents could not afford to buy shoes for school were allowed to attend school barefoot. Many boys and girls alike attended school barefoot; only the richer families could afford to allow their children to wear shoes to school.

In my family, each of us children had only one pair of shoes, and this was only worn on special occasions, so even I attended school barefoot until a man in Christiana opened a factory and started making cheap shoes that almost every one could afford The only problem was that the shoes were made of plastic. They were called "sunflash," and when I got my first pair I was so happy. I could now wear shoes to school.

After a while, almost every child in school had on a "sunflash," but after a few days we learned why they were called "sunflash." You see, when school was on recess and we went outside to play, when the sun got hot and heated the plastic on our feet, it was as if our feet were on fire. To get relief, we would either stay in the shade or take off the "sunflash."

In Jamaica, all school children attending school had to wear uniforms. All schools had a different kind of uniform, so the uniform that I wore to my last school could not be worn to the new school. Also, we could not wear "sunflash" to this new school. We were now getting big; we had to dress differently. My parent had to get new uniforms and new shoes for me to go to school. I could see the worry on mother's face as the beginning of school grew closer. She went to God and prayed, asking God to provide a pair of shoes for me. I could not tell how it happened; the only thing I knew was that one week before I had to report to school, Mother gave me a brand-new pair of shoes for school, the right type for the school, and it fit well.

Here is the story of how I got my shoes, as told by my mother: When she learned that I had to have a pair of sneakers for school, she had no money for this, but for me to go to school, this was a must. So this night she went to God and asked Him for a pair of shoes for him. She prayed, "Dear God, my father, I need a pair of shoes for Curtis to wear to school. Father, if he doesn't get this shoes he can't go to school. Please God, help me. I have no money to buy shoes, but I need it. Please, Lord!'

The next morning, she had an appointment in Spalding (a nearby town). She said that as she was about to take the bus, she heard a voice say, "Do not take the bus; walk." So in obedience to the voice, she walked. As she traveled along, she came to a spot, and the voice said, "Stop. Go off the path and look behind the tree." She obeyed and, to her surprise there was a box behind the tree. She opened it and there was a new pair of shoes.

She was so surprised that she closed the box and went on her way. In the evening, while returning home, she went back to the spot, and it was still there. Once again, she left it and went home. After inquiring of God if this was an answer to her prayer, she sent me for it, telling me where to find it. When I got there, I found it, as she said, and that's how I got my shoes for school.

From this story, you see that God does answer prayers. Even though my mother had asked God for a miracle, it was so hard to believe that God would have worked so fast. This shows God power to do whatever we ask in His name. Look at these scriptures with me. In John 14:13 He says, "And whatever you ask in My name, that I will do." Also, in verse 14, He said, "If you ask anything in My name, I, the Lord will do it." Note that He did not say "may do it," He said He *will*. All we need is faith in God.

GOD PROVIDED FROM ABOVE

This other testimony is from my wife's grandmother in Jamaica. At the time, the country was experiencing a great drought and people were suffering from hunger. She had four children to feed and there was no food. She could hear the children crying for hunger, so she, not knowing what to do, prayed, "Dear God, my family is hungry. I have no food for them. Please help me." She got off her knees and walk outside.

She stood on the steps of the house and looked up and down the road. No help was coming. It seemed as if God did not hear her prayer. Suddenly, she heard a voice in her head saying, "You fool! I keep telling you that there is no God. Now you prayed and you see nothing happen."

She tried to push this voice away, because since childhood she had been learning in church and Sunday School that there was a God and that He made the world and He loved us. As she tried to push the voice away, though, it become more forceful, saying, "There is no God!" Then the youngest child come and held onto her dress. With tears in her eyes, her small voice said, "Mama, I am hungry." With tears in her eyes and the voice of Satan taunting her, she walked to the kitchen. Because most houses in the country had the kitchen built apart from the house, she walked around the kitchen and out into the garden.

Most homes in Jamaica were surrounded by fruit trees, coffee trees, and a kind of vegetable that you will find in almost every home called *cho-cho*. This is often planted at the root of the trees, and its vines grew up all over the top of the trees. If you planted this vegetable where there were no trees, you had to build a harbor or trellis for it to climb. When its season came, it would bear fruit that could be cooked and used in many ways, as meat or as vegetables, depending on how it was prepared.

Even though this was not the season or time for this fruit to be on these vines, she walked into the garden, looking up to see if maybe she may see a *cho-cho* there. She would pick it and cook it for her children. As she walked with her head up and her eyes searching the trees, something fell from the tree, hit her on her hand, and fell to the ground. She looked to see what this was, and saw—lying on the ground at her feet—a penny. Happy to see this, she quickly picked it up, held it up to God, and said, "Thank you, Lord!" She then returned to the yard, called the eldest child, and said, "Go to the shop and buy half pound of cornmeal for me." This money was not enough to buy sugar, but she intended to make some porridge, mix it with salt, and give to the children.

As the child ran off to get the cornmeal, she put the pot on the fire with some water. When the child returned with the meal, she mixed it with water and poured it into the pot. She then began to stir. As she stirred this around and around in the pot, she heard something knocking against the stirring spoon and the side of the pot. She used the spoon to search the bottom of the pot and found that the penny was back! She scooped it out and called the child again and said, "Run to the shop and buy some sugar."

So, she was able to provide food for her children, or should I say, God provided food for the family that day. Here we see God coming through again. What will you call this, a coincidence again, or is God real?

WHEN THE CHILDREN GOT HUNGRY, GOD SENT FOOD

This is another true story that happened in my home, and if you ever get my mother talking, this would be one of her favorite stories of God's quick answer to an earnest prayer. To help prepare your minds for these other great stores of God's miraculous work toward His people, let me take some time to answering some questions that may be troubling you. Also, some of you may have never experienced hunger caused by poverty, but even in America, where there seems to be so much of everything, in my field as a pastor, I have had to deal with this problem very often. We have people around us that go hungry for a number of reasons, but being broke seems to be the main reason. Some people may have jobs, but when they get their paycheck they gamble it away. Others may spend it on drugs, which cause them and their family to suffer. In another case, there is just too little to go around.

Things have improved very much, and so there is much more to go around. In my days, most poor families had to depend on farming to survive, whether it be animal rearing or working the ground. Most of the people in my country, when I was growing up—and I stress "when I was growing up," because things are different today—were very hard-working people, but most times this did not hinder suffering.

For example, the men woke up early in the morning. Their wives also, and she prepared him his breakfast and sometimes something to take along with him to eat during his break. Then, even before the sun rose, he would be off to the field to work the ground and, as I have said before, could be off to help some other farmers in his field. Remember, I had told you about *day-for-day* when my father wanted to add on to our house. This was also done in farming and other kinds of work.

After working so hard, though, if we got a bad season, such as a dry period, then everyone would be in trouble because the seed in the ground needed water to grow. If these seeds stayed too long in the ground and didn't grow, then the seed would spoil, and this would be disastrous, as we would be facing famine and much hunger.

Question two: Pastor, if the weather or if farming was so unpredictable, why didn't the people find some other form of work?

Answer: When I was growing up in Jamaica, only a few good jobs were available, and to work some of the other cheaper jobs didn't really make sense. It was better to try on your own and be self-employed, because not every year was bad for the farmers. If you had a good season, then everyone would be happy. Almost everyone suffered in one way or another. I have been to other countries and found real suffering as well, so let us give thanks for what we have and be happy, and when you can, help someone who seems to be in need.

This was another hard time in Jamaica. My father went to work. We got home from school and saw that there was no cooking going on. We were hungry and tired, but there was no food. I walked into the house and saw my mother just getting off her knees. She walked outside, started the fire, and then turned to us and said, "There is no food in the house, but the Lord told me to put the pot on the fire."

I thought to myself, *What use is that?* She decided not to beg or complain; she could have gone to the neighbors or even to the store and credited something until she could pay for it, but no; today she was going to trust in the Lord. She trusted that he would provide.

As soon as the water in the pot started to boil, there was a call at the gate. There was a little boy coming toward the house with a basket on his head. As he got close, he said, "Good day, Mrs. Peart. Mama sent this for you," and he handed her the basket. It had food and meat, enough to serve for three nights! Is God real or what!

A SIGN THAT I WAS BEING CALLED INTO MINISTRY

At about the age of sixteen, I had another dream. I had always been seeing signs that maybe the Lord was calling me into ministry, but this dream was so real. I dreamed that I went to visit a church just across town. When I walked in, the place was filled with people. I found a seat in the back and sat down. Everybody was waiting for the preacher, but there was none. Suddenly, I was on the rostrum standing around the pulpit.

I don't remember walking up there, but as I stood there, I saw a bright angel sitting on a cross beam over the audience and a bright light came from the face of the angel and shone right at me. I felt something going through me, and suddenly I was like a machine. Words came pouring out of me, and I was preaching to this crowd. When I woke out of my sleep, I was confused; I couldn't understand what the Lord was saying or doing with me, but this I knew: I must submit myself to His will. You see, the Lord has many ways to speak to His people, and this was how He chose to speak to me.

Our church organization allowed foreign preachers to visit the work in Jamaica, and oftentimes they would visit some of our churches. One missionary met me one day and said, "There is a mark on you; you are going to be a preacher. Promise me you will go to Bible School and be trained. You are going to be a preacher.

BEING SICK, ALMOST TO DEATH

I continued living my life as normal as ever. One day, something very dreadful happened; I suddenly became very sick. I was sixteen at the time. My body was covered with watery boils from my head to my feet. This was very painful, so I cried night and day. I wanted to die, and so, in my pain and itching, I prayed, "Lord, please take my life from me." Yes, it was better to die than to suffer so much. I prayed, "Lord, what have I done to You that You allow this suffering to come upon me?"

What made things worse was that when I cried to God for help, He never answered me. One day in my suffering, Satan came to me and said, "God doesn't hear you, and He never will, but if you trust me and promise to work for me, I will help you." Even though I was suffering, I shouted, "Satan, I rebuke you in the name of Jesus!" and went back to crying and nursing my wounds.

I could see that my parents were worried. They tried all the home remedies they knew, but my sickness just got worse. I couldn't sleep at nights; I couldn't sleep by day. When my parents saw that there was nothing they could do, they took me to one doctor then another. They both gave different views. They too were confused; they did not know what was happening to me. After the doctors, I just got worse. I often stood at the window of our house with not much hope of getting better, tears in my eyes, and a lot on my mind. I missed school. I missed playing with my friends. I could not go to church, though sometimes my pastor and others from the church came by to visit me. I looked forward to their visit, but after they left, I went back to my old self. I wanted to die so that all this would be over, but I just lived on.

One day, I was taken back to the doctor. He told my mom that there was something wrong with my heart, and I may not live to see my seventeen birthday. This was not good news to them; no parent, no matter how sick their child is, wants to hear that their child is going to die. For me, I never cared if I lived or died. To me, dying was better; I would be set free from my pain.

Again I stood by my window, my eyes focusing on the winding road that came from the main road to our house. It was as if I was expecting something or someone to come up this path. After a while, I thought I saw something moving. Yes, someone was coming. As the person came up the path to our house, I could see that it was a man dressed in clean but funny clothes.

As he came into the yard, he called out hello. My mother hurried to see who it was. The man, after introducing himself, said, "I came to see your son who is sick." My mom took him to see me. Looking at me, he said, "Son, the Lord has sent me to you. The Lord said to tell you that He heard your cry, but don't worry about what the doctor said." Then he prayed for me and said, "You are healed. Keep serving God. Never stray from His path, and you will be okay." Then, he said good-bye and was gone.

A little while after his visit, my boils started to dry up, and in a few days, I was better. After my healing, I must confess that I never really believed what the doctor said. He had said that I had a boil on my heart, and he was unable to do anything about it. He said that when it burst, I would die. Looking back now, I must confess that perhaps the doctor was right. I think it was about 1997 when I felt a pain in my chest. It became so severe that I went to the doctor to get it checked out. The doctors believed that this was a sign of a heart attack and ran many tests, which all came out negative.

After the exams, the doctor said they found a spot on my heart that showed that some time, long ago, I had suffered some damage to part of my heart, but that it was nothing for me to worry about because it was very old. He said it must have happened many years ago, because the wound had healed, but they could still see the scar. I then remembered what the doctor said to me as a child in Jamaica and when the man who prayed for me said I was healed. It was all true. Yes, my dear friends; I am a walking miracle. I was going to die in my early teens, but God healed me. Is God real or what? As I think of this, I feel like shouting "Hallelujah!" I am now fifty-three years old and still going strong.

You see, when man gives up, God does not. My friends, if you've been to the doctor and was told that there is nothing more that can be done for you, turn your troubles over to the Lord and you'll see. When your mother, father, brother, sister, preacher, judge, and even lawyers fail you, God will never fail. Why not trust Him today, and you will see that I am telling the truth.

I am hoping that as I go on with my testimonies that your faith in God will be so lifted that you will do as John 14:14 says, "And if you ask any thing in My name I will do it." You will be able to ask of the Lord and see it done. He also said in Matthew 21:21 and 22, "If you have faith and doubt not, ye shall not only cause a tree to dry up, but if you shall say to this mountain, 'Be thou removed and be cast into the sea,' it shall be done. And all things, whatsoever ye shall ask in prayer believing, ye shall receive." Do you have faith to be blessed today? It's all up to you.

Remember, I said before that the last thing I wanted to be was a pastor, but one year, the Pentecostal Church of God planned a crusade at the national stadium in Kingston, Jamaica. It was a very good campaign; almost all of the Pentecostal churches throughout the island came to join the American missionaries for this campaign. It was here that a missionary walked over to me, reached out and took my hand, and said, "The Lord will use you as a pastor. You must go to Bible school when the time comes. Yes, my brother, I can see the mark on you."

I think of these words sometimes but never really put this to practice. In 1986, everything began as if it were a dream: My mother and pastor talked together about me going to Bible college. Mom went and spoke to my dad, and they all agreed that I should enter Bible School. You see, my dad was not a hard man to deal with; if you approached him in the right way, he would agree with you.

So, it was soon agreed that I could go to Bible school. My pastor came to me and encouraged me to register for Bible school one morning in September. It was like a dream; I found myself standing on the campus of the Caribbean Pentecostal College compound. I thought to myself, "What in the world am I doing here?" But yes, my friends, here I was. I didn't know if I could manage a college education because, while attending public school, I was never a bright guy, but I was here and now everything was left in the hand of God. I approached my task with fear; what would happen, I don't know.

Bible college turned out to be fun. I settled down and really studied. I also discovered some undiscovered talent in me; I realized that I had the ability to improve my educational standard, so after six months in college I completely lost my fear and started to do better than I thought I could. So many people give up before even trying, but I learned that you should never give up before you at least try. Proverbs 24:16 says, "The just man falleth seven times and riseth again, but the wicked shall fall into mischief." If everyone was like this, what would happen to the world? God wants us to try and try again.

Let me tell you a story. I came to this country in April 1983. I did not really want to come because back home I was a pastor and my church brethren were like family to me. I wanted to stay with them, but at the same time, my own family was in America—my mother, father, sisters and brothers. I was the only one left in Jamaica out of my family, and I longed to see them. When my family in America invited me to join them, I expressed to them my desire, and they agreed that I could stay in Jamaica, but I must visit them every year.

When I told this to the immigration office, they refused to give me a visitor's visa to go back and forth; they said the only visa they were willing to give me was a full stay in the country of America, and it had to be for my whole family, meaning my wife and children. When I told this to my family in America, they demanded that I apply for permanent stay so the family could be together. So I did, and we all—my wife and three kids—were granted permanent stay in this country.

On my arrival, a job was already waiting for me through the influence of my mother and a dear church sister, Mrs. Brown, who was living in an apartment complex called Tracy's Towers at the time. She was the one who sought a job for me as a part of the security team for the building where she lived. She was such a great woman. Every day she prepared lunch for me, and when I offered her some money to help she refused to take it. She respected me and treated me like her own son. Eventually, she became a part of my congregation.

My job was not permanent; I worked as a stand-by security guard. This meant that if someone did not show up to work, I was called in, so I got less work than the others. My wife also found a job in Manhattan, in a distribution warehouse, where she did packing. Her net pay was one hundred and fifty dollars per week, and from this pay, twenty dollars was used on transportation. We had a small apartment. My wife worked during the day while I prepared the children and sent them off to school. I took mostly night jobs, so that when she got home in the evenings, I went off to work.

On my job, we got paid on Wednesday evening, but by Saturday, some of my fellow workers would come to me borrowing money, because all their money was finished and they couldn't even buy lunch for themselves.

One day, one of them came to me and asked, "Do you have an apartment?"

"Yes," I said.

"How many are in your household?" he asked.

"Five," I replied.

"I don't understand," he said. "In my household, there is just me and my wife and one son. Every week, I receive more money than you do. How do you do it? Every week, as soon as I get paid, my money is finished, but you always have money to lend us. How do you do it?"

"I give to the Lord," I said. "I try not to live above my means, and, with God's help, I make it." This in our twenty-ninth year in America, and we have never applied to the government for any form of help. Yet, we bought a house. We own two cars, though not new. My wife owns her own car, though. I also went to school and improved my education. So did my wife, who got herself a good job. Living independently here is my answer. No one owes you anything; it is all left up to your ambition. What's your ambition? I can remember my wife telling me that as she got out of the subway and tried to push through the snow to get to her job, she fell down and had to get up, dust herself off with tears in her eyes, and go to her job. I can hear many of you saying, "I would not do it," but we both know that we had bills to pay, food to buy, and children to care for, so we had to work.

I can remember days, as I ran to work, after bringing the children to school, when I would see young men and women and sometimes even older people standing idly by the side of the road sitting on the park benches doing nothing. The Bible says, "Why stand ye idle? Find some work to do." I can remember one day, this man walked up to me and said, "Beg you something." When I asked him why he was not working, he said, "I can't find any work."

Feeling sorry for him because he said he was hungry, I gave him some money and told him if he come and see me tomorrow

I would give him a job. I waited but he never showed. I then concluded that some people do not want to work, but when they see a working person succeed, they envy them and may even kill to get what they didn't work for.

Now that I have finally made it in life, I sometimes see some of these same people in the same spot on the park benches and in the same condition. Proverbs 26:15-16 says, "The slothful hideth his hand in his bosom and it grieveth him to bring it to his mouth again."

BEING A PASTOR WHILE ATTENDING SCHOOL

While in Bible school, because we were studying for the ministry, we were allowed to go out on some weekends and preach in other churches. Sometimes, I would go back to my home church. My pastor was a pioneer and sometimes would take some of the brethrens from his church and go out looking for new areas to start a new church. Any new work that started outside of the main church was called an out-station. They had to depend on the mother church to take care of them until they were big enough to take care of themselves. When it reached this level, it would be called a church.

Our church started an out-station in a district called Hibernia. It was often left unattended, so my pastor saw this as the right place to send me to try out my pastorship. There was another church brother who went to school with me, and my pastor decided to send us both out to Hibernia. We would go to that place to pastor every weekend. This turned out to be good for this new church; it started to grow rapidly.

We would go up to Hibernia on Saturday and board with an old man we nicknamed Mas. Mocha. He was a very holy man who loved the Lord and who was a member of the church. Although he was much older than us, he respected us as his pastors. He even shared his bed with us, so we would sleep head to foot on one bed.

The church was held in a big car garage that the home church rented and paid for, since we were not yet able to carry on our own. Although our being in Hibernia was an asset to the district, there were still some people who would prefer that we were not there. As the church grew, many young people who used to roam the streets and make trouble were now coming to church, but this also affected the big churches around.

They made it known that they did not like having us around, but that did not stop us. We were young and enthusiastic, and I think this helped to draw the youth to the church. Another person who never cared to have us in the district was the dance hall owner. You see, in Jamaica when a person became a follower of Christ, he or she held their Christianity very serious and saw attending dance halls as a big sin.

The owner of the dance hall was upset with us because we were taking away his patrons. Also, we were located in the square, right next to the dance hall. The owner of the clubs started turning the people of the community against us, but the more they fought, the more the church grew. This was a "hot" little church, and many mothers and fathers came and made this their church. The size of the church helped a lot in this fight because since we were strangers in this district, standing by ourselves would have been hard, but with so many people of the district joining us it made us stronger and we soon become a force to be reckoned with. After a while, the dance hall owner changed his tactics. Every time we started to have service, he would put on his music. He would put on his sound system and completely drown out our church service.

One night, we were having church. God was really moving: people were being healed. The crowd got so big that some people had to climb up in the ceiling to see the movement of God. I was full of power; Brother Grant, my assistant, was full of power. God was working through him, and many were being baptized with the Holy Spirit. Some people were lying flat on the ground; some had their hands lifted in worship of God.

Then, this man decided to break up our service. He put on his music and turned it up very high. I was in the Spirit, and I took the microphone, stretched my right hand toward the dance hall, and cursed it in the name of Jesus. I said, "In the name of Jesus, music mash up (meaning be destroyed)!" Instantly, we heard *conk-conkey-conk*, and everything stopped. From that night on, no more music played there again, because the whole system was destroyed.

Eventually, that dance hall was turned into a meat shop, and fear fell on the people who saw what happened. The saints worshiped God even more. Ironically, the owner of the dance hall was said to be a member of one of the outstanding nominal churches in the area. The man from whom we rented the place where we kept our meetings was also from one of these churches.

One day, without warning, I received a written notice to evacuate the building. This was something we were not ready for; there was no other place around where we could move the church, so this was a big problem. We decided to go and have a talk with this gentleman, but before we went, we joined hands together and prayed for God's guidance.

After prayer, I went to the man's home. His wife met me at the door and invited me in. The gentleman, his wife, and I had a long talk. He told me that even though he belonged to another church, he was very glad that we came to the district because since we came, there had been such a change, even in the youths. However, he said he was being pressured to evict us. He did not tell me by whom, but I understood very well. Nonetheless, before I left he assured me that we did not have to move. Feeling very happy, I thanked him, and left. From that time on, we have been good friends.

When I returned and gave the news to the church, everyone gave a happy shout of praise to the Lord because he had come through for us one more time. Can you imagine the joy we felt when we knew that we didn't have to worry anymore about moving, and, more than that, we were reassured that we could stay as long as we had to? To God is all the praise!

Two years after I started school, I left school on Friday and went to Hibernia. The church had so many young people that I decided to start a youth program in the church. So, after talking it over with my pastor and the president of the Bible school, we all agreed that it was a good idea to start a program that would allow the youths to become more involved. We decided to have it on Friday nights, so I went the following Friday. Everything went well that night, and the youths were very enthusiastic and happy that we were willing to make time for them.

After church, I went to Bro. Griffith's house, the same man we nicknamed "Mocha," the place we boarded whenever we went to Hibernia. As always, I was received with joy. I stayed the night and decided that, since Bro. Grant and I had to be back on Saturday night to help with the church for Sunday, it did not make much sense to go back to school and then come back in the evening. I decided that I would just stay. Also, I often had to walk from Hibernia to school, which was about a ten-mile journey, so it was better to stay.

On Saturday, with nothing else to do, I spent most of the day studying. I got so engrossed in my studies that I lost track of the time. It wasn't until I heard my stomach growling that I realized that I hadn't eaten, and I became very hungry. However, I was so involved in my studies that I did not want to go out and get food. I paused for a while, thinking of what to do, and then I remembered that my God is ever-present, and as a good friend, He cares about me. So I spoke to Him, saying, "Father, I am hungry." Instantly He spoke back to me.

"What do you want to eat?" He asked.

"I need a pineapple soda with bun and cheese. When You send it, Lord, let them cut the bun and put the cheese inside." I then went back to my studies. In a little while, there was a knock on the door and someone was standing there with a pineapple soda and a bun with the cheese inside. Since I asked for it, I took it, said thanks, and went back to my studies. Is God real or what!

My school became concerned that I would get too caught up with this new program that I would not have as much time for my studies and might fail. However, after much consideration, they decided to allow me to try this out for a while, but I was warned that if I show any sign of falling back in my schoolwork, then we had to come up with a new plan. I agreed because I did not want to stop going to this place. I loved these people so much.

To everyone's surprise, I did very well in school, so much so that I even surprised myself. You may remember that I said I did not do well in public school, and so I was not too sure that I could manage college work. I know that this had to be God because, even though I was not the brightest one in school, I was passing my tests and, even though I know my teachers would like to see more from me, for the time being they seemed to be satisfied with my efforts.

After a while, going to Hibernia on Fridays and staying until Sunday became a routine, and I started doing this every week. My partner wasn't doing so well with studies, so most of the time I had to go there by myself. I would do this every week, except when we were having some special test, when I would then go on Fridays, stay until Monday morning, and, most times, walk to school.

One Monday, I left Hibernia at about eleven-thirty. I had my bag containing my schoolbooks because, while in the field, whenever I had some free time I had to study. This was a part of my agreement with my school. I put my bag on my shoulder, said good-bye, and started on my journey. As I walked, I became hungry, thirsty, and tired. My steps became slow. I had been walking a long time, about three miles. It was now about midday, and the road was so hot you could almost see the steam coming up out of it. As I walked, I tried my best to stay in the shade of the trees, which only helped for a little while, because I eventually had to go right back into the sun.

Sometimes the cloud would cover the sun, and for a little while I felt some form of relief, but very soon I was right back where I was before. I thought, "Oh my God, I can't make it." I felt very weak. I knew that it would not be too long before I fainted. I had no money for a cab and no money for the bus. If I had, then I would stand and wait, but I had none. I had been walking for some time now, but I was still far away from school. I knew the devil was having a field day watching me as I struggled, because I could hear him mocking me.

I felt like putting down my heavy bag and just sit for a while, but I knew that would not be wise. It would look disgusting for a preacher to be sitting by the wayside. Once again, Satan came mocking and jeering me. He said, "Isn't it a shame? You say you are a preacher working for the Lord. Last night you were telling the people to have faith in God; now you need help, and where is He?"

All the time, when Satan attacked me, I paid him no attention. He would come and speak some word of discouragement to me and then stand back to see what I was going to do or say. I tried to communicate with God in my mind. I was happy to know that He could have found someone better than I to do His work, but instead He had chosen me, so I counted it a privilege to be suffering for Him. Please don't consider me a fool; I knew what I am saying. I can hear some of you saying, "Who could be glad for suffering!" but I do hope you will understand that I am not saying I enjoyed suffering, but that, if it came to it, I would gladly suffer for Him.

I was thinking of this when suddenly something Satan said seemed to knock me to my senses. He said, "Where is your God?"

It was as if I was lost and now I found my way; it was as if I was blind and suddenly my eyes popped open, as if a light just broke in my head and now I could see. "Where is your God?" he said.

I stopped right where I was, turned my head upwards, and said, "Daddy, You call me Your son. I am working for You. Now here I am weary and tired. Do You expect me to walk all the way to school in this weary state?" I put my bag down and said, "If You don't send me help then I am stopping right here and I will not move any further."

Just then, a car stopped by me, and the man who was driving looked at me and said, "Come in." I took my bag and went in. He took me all the way to school. I thanked him, and he returned back the way we came. Seeing him going back the way we just came helped me confirm the fact. This is the Lord at work. This doesn't happen much in my country. Someone going out of their way to pick up a stranger on the street, and take me home? No, this was God answering my cry for help. I lifted my head to God and said, "thank you," and went to my room.

I must say that I was not surprised at the fast way the Lord answers prayer, because that's what He said in His Word, the Bible: "Call on Me and I will answer." In Psalm 107:28-30, it says, "Then they cry unto the Lord in their trouble, and He bringeth them out of their distresses;.... then are they glad because they be quiet; so He bringeth them unto their desired haven. Oh, that man would praise the Lord for His goodness, and for His wonderful works to the children of men." James 1:3 also says, "Knowing this that the trying of your faith worketh patience;" Hebrews 10:35 says, "Cast not away therefore your (faith) or confidence which hath great recompense of reward"; and Mark 11:24 says, "Whatsoever you desire, when you pray, believe that ye receive them, and ye shall have them."

Notice what happened here; it took Satan's mocking voice to bring me to my senses.

I am sure that if the devil had known this would happen, he would not have tried this with me. My friends, when it seems there is no way out, when your way seems dark as night, trust in God; He never fails. Read Psalm 27:11, which says, "Teach me Thy way, oh Lord, and lead me in a plain part." Learn this, my friends: since you turned from the devil and came to God, your life has changed. Satan does not know you anymore; he only remembers what you use to be, what you use to love, the things you use to do. This is to his disadvantage. He doesn't know you any more, so stop complaining; he is listening to you, and you will give him a way to get into your life—to his detriment, though, as this will only help to strengthen you.

You see, it seems that when the devil was in heaven, before God cast him out (Revelation 12:7), he was a very powerful angel. According to Isaiah 14:12, he knew a lot of things, was able to go a lot of places in God's kingdom, and had great powers, so much so that he was lifted up with pride and started to set himself up as God. You can read his intention in verses 13 and 14 of Isaiah 14.

However, when he was cast out of heaven, he lost some of his great power. Let me prove to you that Satan does not know all things. In Matthew 2:7-12, we see that Satan planned to kill Jesus through Herod, but somehow God gave Satan the slip, and Jesus was brought to Egypt, out of the reach of Herod. Next, the devil made a very big mistake when he caused the death of Christ. If you read Psalms 24:7-10, Revelation 5, and Revelation 1:17-18, you will see what I mean. After the death of Jesus, he was defeated and lost most of his power. If he had known this would happen, he would most likely fight to keep Jesus alive, but he made a big blunder when he had Him killed. Because of the death of Jesus, we will gain eternal life; we are redeemed by His shed blood. This means it was a good thing when Christ died on the cross.

We don't have to be afraid of the devil any more, because Christ fought him for us and gave us the victory. I will also say without any reservation that whoever tries to make Satan a God can't be right. God must be omnipresent, which means able to be everywhere at the same time, but Satan is not (read Proverbs 15: 3, Proverbs 30: 4, Psalms 139:7–13, Matthew 25:31–46, Deuteronomy10:14, 1 Chronicles 29:11, and Psalms 24:1). Satan is not God. If he were, sinners would have it much harder to turn from a life of sin and turn to Jesus as Savior because, whether we want to accept it are not, Satan has some power and he is very cunning; he is able to convince men to stay in sin (Ezekiel 28:13 and 1 Peter 5:8), but we are saved through the power of the gospel and the blood of the Lamb.

Likewise, no one can be God without omniscience, meaning knowing all things (Job 12:22-24 and 1:26. 6, Psalms 33:13 and 33:1). Satan does not know all things.

A God must also be omnipotent, meaning all powerful (Psalms 115:3 and Matthew19:26); Satan is not. If he was, he would not be about to be chained in utter darkness for a thousand years, as we learn will happen to him (Revelations 20:1-3). This would not happen to him if he was God. If he was, there is no way he would have been chained in darkness for thousands of years. Revelations 20:1-3 explains this further.

LET'S TALK ABOUT SCHOOL

Many people ask what it was like attending Bible school. School was fun, and I think we could call it a home away from home. Even though we had a lot of hard studies, we also had a lot of good fun too.

The name of our school was the Caribbean Pentecostal College, located in Manchester, Jamaica. I can remember my first day in college. Everyone was happy to see me. I was certainly not a stranger to any of my fellow students and the teachers, because even before coming to school here, we had met in conventions, fellowship meetings, rallies, concerts, and many others places; we were somehow already acquainted, and so they came and told me how happy they were to see me in school.

On Monday night, Brother Steve, the gardener, came to me and welcomed me and told me that Thursday night would be initiation night. Since this was my first time in college, I had not heard of such a night. I asked him what he meant by initiation night, and he said it's a night set apart when we introduce ourselves to each other, and this was going to take place every Thursday night until we all understood each other. I became very curious, mostly because of the sound of his voice and the look on his face when he talked; he seemed to be enjoying it.

In a funny way, I felt that this could be something I wouldn't enjoy. There were other new students that started with me. They too had received the message and were as concerned as I was. What was this initiation? We all wanted to know. One thing I was sure about was that this could not be something bad. After all, this was Bible school, and everyone here was supposed to be a Christian. We were here to study for the ministry, so we were serious people on the Lord's work. Therefore, there should be no idleness, no fighting, no quarreling; all were supposed to be good, so why worry? No matter how much I tried, though, something kept troubling my mind, so all the new students got together and decided that we had to find out what this was.

We went to one of the more advanced students who was in his second year and inquired of him the meaning of initiation day. He told us that Thursday nights we would all be commanded to strip naked. Everyone had to do it—both old and new students had to remove all of their clothes. The light would be turned off, all doors would be locked.

He said the best thing to do was to find a good hiding place, because they will be searching in the dark, and if they see a shadow moving in the dark, it would be attacked. At this point, everyone would come out of hiding with belts, and the beating would begin. Everyone could decide to hit just the new person with the belt or hit each other. This was a form of initiation done every time a new student came to the dorm. This was their way of saying welcome.

I did not like the sound of this, so I said I wouldn't do this, and almost all of us new students agreed that we wouldn't participate. The older student said that on Thursday night, the rules would be read, and everyone must do what you were ordered or else the rules would be changed for the night, and everyone would come down on you and beat you.

I could not believe what I was hearing. Although I did not like the sound of this, when I thought about it, it sounded like fun. Before the day was over, I was ready if this was part of college. I had to be ready because what could we do? We had to live together, and since this involved everyone, it did not sound too bad. After all, they had belts, but I had a belt too; I might be beaten as well as I might have the opportunity to beat someone. This was fair; this was equal opportunity.

Soon, the night of our initiation came. Everything seemed normal until about nine o'clock, just as we were getting ready for bed. Suddenly, the announcement was made by Brother Steve. "Brothers," he said, "it's so good that we are all here, but we must make our newcomers feel welcome. Here is how we will do it: We will all strip down to our underwear and get a belt in hand. Then, I will turn the light out, and the rest is up to you."

After inspection, to ensure that we were all in compliance with the rules, the lights went out. This was fun. You could see everyone running to find a safe place to hide. In my hand, I had a real thick belt that I got from my brother, Milton, and I hid behind a cabinet. Some people were under the bunks; some hid under the table; some in the bathroom and any other place you could hide.

From my hiding place, I saw a shadow moving about in the dark. As he moved about, he was feeling on the beds and searching under the beds. From his shape and built in the dark, I realized that this was Steve. This was how it worked. We couldn't stay hidden all night; someone had to be brave enough to come out of hiding and get the show on the way, so Steve decided to be the one. I remained hidden, not daring to make a sound that would give my hiding place away and have him pull me out. So I remained still, watching him as he moved about looking for his first victim.

Suddenly, he started coming my way! I held my breath, but he turned away to investigate a sound coming from the closet. With his back now turned to me, I saw my chance to strike, so I silently crept out of my hiding place with my belt in hand, walked up to Steve, and give him three hits with the belt.

As soon as I started, everyone came out of hiding, and you could hear the sound of the belts. The whole dorm was filled with laughter; it was as if a group of children was at play. Next, we had to get busy and clean up because pillows, which were also used in the fight as shields, had shed feathers all over the place.

The next day, this was the only talk on the campus. We laughed at those who showed signs of much beating. We, the newcomers, soon found out that this was not meant to cost us any hurt but rather to bring some fun in our lives. After all, "too much study and no play make Jack a dull boy."

When I use to hear about Bible school, I thought the only study was Bible studies, but I soon found out that it was not so. Instead, we had to do mathematics, courses in English, Spanish, and history, and your grades could not be lower than 65 percent. In addition, we had to study religion. This was our main lesson and covered with topics such as church history, old and new testament survey, life of the apostles, life of Christ, physiology, biology, Kingdom of the Cults, the facts about evolution, and survey of the Bible, just to name a few. And I soon learned that we have to pass all our subjects before we could graduate; if anyone fails one subject, you have to repeat another year.

I remember sometimes having to study for four tests because we would be having four tests in one day. I can also remember things getting so mixed-up in my mind that what I thought was going to be on one teacher's test ended up on another's. Now, thinking back and comparing my studies in Jamaica to my studies in America, Jamaica was much harder. For example, I remember studying for our final exam in Church History when our teacher came to class and told us that we must study the complete textbook, and that if we failed this test we would be held back for another year. When we heard this, we all buckled down and really studied for this test.

When the day of the tests came, as we took each test and finished, we breathed a sigh of relief. By the time lunchtime came, we had finished three tests. We had one hour for lunch break, but for many of us all that was on our mind was this last test that could cause us to repeat another year in school. So we had a short lunch and took the time to refresh our memories. This was easier to do, since we only had one last test to worry about for that day. We could now put all your energies into studying for this test.

When it was time for us to go back to class, I was so sure that I could pass this test. I thought I knew the book so much I could sing it to you. Yes, I was ready for my test. The teacher entered the room with a little grin on his face as if to say "I've got you." He walked to the front of the room and holding up the test, he said, "Well, class, you have it easy today; you have one question, with the value of one hundred points." Even after seventeen years I can still remember the question: "In what year did Constantinople fall and explain in detail why."

Oh, we were so upset! We had wasted our time preparing for a big test and now look what we got? A question we were not thinking would be on the test became the only question of the whole subject. We just sat and looked at each other. What did our teacher just do to us? I tried my best and got a score of sixty, thus failing. To my surprise, every one failed, and so we all had to stay for another year.

In the days, weeks, and even months that followed, every one I met on campus was talking about what happened with the test. To many of us, we had already spent two long years studying and we were looking toward our graduation, but here we were facing another long year of school. We had our finals in April and were hoping to graduate in June, but now we felt so disappointed. Most of us did well on all the other tests, and now we couldn't graduate because of one failed test. However, we soon found out that it did not make any sense to agonize over this. The principal wasn't about to change his mind, so we had to put this behind us and just move on.

Since the finals were over, we could pretty much do anything we wanted to do—lay idly around the campus, sleep if we felt like it, anything. I can remember one day Steve came to us and told us that we were going to do a cookout. This was Friday, and he just got paid and he wanted to give us a treat. So, he went to the meat shop and bought some beef, flour, and all that was needed to make soup. Yes, this was what he was about to cook for us: beef soup. We were happy to know that we were going to get some food in the evening, because almost every night we got hungry. Lunch was served at twelve o'clock and supper at five o' clock, so you know by the night we were hungry.

This was a common thing to do on Fridays in Jamaica. They would slaughter the cow or other animal, and people would come to the slaughterhouse to buy their meat. After the health inspector inspected and passed the meat as good, he would stamp it, and then the meat could be sold and eaten. If all this meat was not sold on the spot, then the rest would be sold to the country stores or taken to the market and be sold on Saturday, the big shopping day. If they killed the animal and sold it before it was inspected, the butcher could be charged a big fine in court or even go to jail.

So, this was where Steve went and got the meat. Now, the only way we could participate in this cookout was if we got permission from the principal. If he said no, then we couldn't join the cookout. Steve, on the other hand, could do anything he wanted to, because he was not a student; he worked there, so he controlled the running of the place. He was also a member of the campus church, so this increased his privilege. He also oversaw our activities in the field. One of our duties was to work in the field. We would plant things for the school to use as food, and if we cultivated more than we could use, then the street sellers would come and buy it and take it to the market.

So, we went to the principal and asked if we could join this cookout, and we were told yes. We stopped at the girls' dorm and gave them the good news and promised to bring their food to them when it was ready. After that evening, it became a routine; almost every Friday night Steve would be cooking for us, and we could look forward to yam, dumpling, and other things to eat.

One day, the cooking began late, because Steve went out and came back late. He came and asked if we still wanted him to cook for us. We wanted to, but we had to ask permission because the food would be late. We went and asked, and were given the ok. The only thing was that we could not join Steve in the cooking. The cooking took much longer than expected this time because this meat was tough and much harder to cook.

The evening went by and the food was still not ready. Steve told us the problem and we all understood; we were willing to wait. Then suddenly we heard a knock on the door. It was the principal! We knew whenever he came to the dorm there was trouble. "Boys," he said. "I will not allow you guys to eat at such late hours."

So he went to Steve and told him no food for the student; it was too late for them to eat. You see, the principal was not a Jamaican, and he did not know that we Jamaicans can eat any time, night or day, and nothing would happen to us. So, Steve came to us and asked what he should do with the food. It was already cooked, and it could not stay until the next day. Someone had to eat it, so we decided to have it. Who would know? We told Steve to bring the food to the dorm; we were going to hide and eat. If while we are eating and the principal came to check again, we would hide it, but we would not allow good food to waste. Steve brought the whole pot of food to the dorm, and, as we always did whenever we had food, we shared it with the female students because they too were hungry. Because it was now dark, it was easy for us to sneak it to them. They also knew that we were forbidden to eat this food, so they too had to hide and eat.

We got plates from the kitchen and began to eat. However, something very dreadful happened among the student body. We had two small guys in our cohort; we called one "Peewee" and the other "Indian." These two did not get along and often got into arguments. One moment, all was well and the other moment they were fighting about something. On this night when we were hiding, they had a disagreement, and without warning Peewee grabbed the pot of food and turned it over in the dorm, making a mess.

Even though this was bad, we had to laugh. The next day, you could see food all over the place; we had to clean up before the principal saw it. So, after all, we did not eat that night. We had to take these two boys and rebuke them; they were supposed to be Christians. We had to help them.

I am happy to say that nothing like that happened again. One of my reasons for telling this story is for a laugh, but the other is to show that in the best of us, there is weakness. Even though we were all here studying to be ministers, there were some weak ones among us, and when we found them we had to give them help so that they could grow in the Lord. Not everyone who seems to be an angel is an angel, and if you keep your eyes on man instead of on God, you will become discouraged and fall out of the way. We must keep our eyes on Jesus.

Well, a few days after this incident, things were back to normal. Now each day after classes, we would have dinner and then go to our chores. Yes, we had chores; the girls had to wash our clothes and help to cook. We the guys work the field and help to keep the yard clean. The work was hard; we dug the soil, weeded the grass, and planted the food. Sometimes we were tired and hungry; in the daytime, the sun was hot, and we had to work in it, so we often got weary. We had to do this, though, because this was also one of the rules. Because this was hard work, some of us soon found ways to keep from going to work in the field. For example, we would fast.

We did not mind missing breakfast so that we could go on fasting, and when we were fasting we were not expected to work. So we fasted from morning past our work time, and when it was dinner time, we would break our fast and be around the dinner table. Soon the principal found out that we were fasting to skip work in the field, so he gave an order that, whether we were fasting are not, we had to work in the field. Not long after, we stopped fasting because it was hard to fast and work in the field.

Now the campus was filled with many fruit trees: oranges, tangerines, grapefruits, and many other fruits. So, while working, we would pick an orange or so and eat. Soon we received an order that we could not eat the oranges, so we made a plan: We went to the camp manager and asked if we could eat the fruits that had fallen to the ground, and he said yes. This is what we wanted to hear, so each time we went to the field, we would hold the trees and have shaking contests. Oranges went flying everywhere. We would not eat them the same day, but the next day when we got to the field there would be oranges for everyone.

They should have allowed us to eat what we wanted because now more oranges and other fruits were being wasted. Anyway, this did not last too long. It seemed as if we were being watched, because one day the manager came to us and said we must pick up the oranges off the ground and take them to the storeroom. We stopped shaking them off after that. This proves that even though we were studying for the ministry, we had our shortcomings.

Nevertheless, everyone still had be careful what we were doing because in this area, people around know that this was a Bible school, and the people studying here are supposed to be to be Christians. Remember, the word "Christian" really means Christlike, so when there was a fight or quarrel, we tried to diffuse them right away and often gave the parties sharp rebukes. This had great effects, and the culprits would withdraw and think of the wrong they had done.

A YOUNG GIRL SAVED FROM RAPE AND MAYBE DEATH

While attending Bible school, the students could go home on the weekends. One weekend, I said good-bye to my fellow students and faculty and set off for home. When I arrived, everyone was happy to see me and welcomed me with opened arms. I had walked all the way home, about five miles, so by the time I got home it was already getting dark.

Suddenly, the same urgency I had to go see my family returned. Now, I wanted to go out on the street. I had no reason to want to walk the street; this was very strange. I just walked from school and my feet were tired. I should want to rest, but I felt as if I had to go out on the street. But why? There was nothing there—no stores, no place of interest, nothing. I went to my mother and said, "Mom, I will be back soon."

"Where are you going?" she asked.

"I don't know. I just feel I have to go out on the street." She, like any good mother, started to protest.

"You just came and you must be tired. Where could you want to go at this hour? You must be crazy." She protested but never said I should not go, so up the hill I went, and out on the street. As I walked, I noticed something funny: there was a young girl walking alone, and she seemed to be afraid of something. I could tell by her behavior.

As I drew closer, she approached a maul hole—the place they had dug out in the hill to find a soft stone that, when grounded, was used to make concrete. This hole was much bigger than the one I told you about earlier in the book; here, instead of using their hands, the workers had used bulldozers to make the hole.

In your mind, imagine bulldozers digging in to a hillside and big dump trucks pulling into this quarry and removing maul and stone for five years. In Jamaica, everyone refers to this as a maul hole. So, this maul hole was left unattended for a long time, and it had become overgrown with bushes and weed.

I was walking on the left side of the road, and she was on the right. As I got closer to her, I could see why she looked so afraid; two men with their pants foot rolled up were not too far behind her. I could see that these men were up to no good. I stopped and watched. As the girl approached the maul hole, they quickened their steps, grabbed hold of her, and began pulling her into the bushes toward the maul hole.

She began to cry out for help, but one of the men covered her mouth with one hand while holding firmly onto her left side. The other man lifted her off the ground and proceeded to carry her toward the maul hole. What should I do? At a time like this, when I needed help, there was no one around. I knew that I could not run over and help her; they might kill me, and I couldn't run off and get help, because it might be too late for her.

I had to do something, so at the top of my voice I called out "Let her go! Let her go!"

I began jumping up and down, shouting at the top of my voice. When they saw that I wasn't going anywhere and that I intended to shout until help came, they let her go and ran away. When I saw that the way was clear, I went over to her. They had started ripping her clothes from her. She was shaking with fear. I asked her if she was okay and if she wanted me to get the police. She said no.

"I think you should report it," I protested. "They might try it with someone else who may not be so lucky." Trembling, she still said no.

"I have a headache," she said. I gave her some money to buy some painkillers, because she would be passing a store. I offered to walk her home, but she said she can make it on her own. As she went on her way, I stayed for a while to make sure that she was not been followed, and then I went home. I was used that night to save this girl's life!

I went home and told my family what happened. They were amazed. Can't you see that God is good?

I spent the rest of the weekend with my family, and my spirit was relaxed within me.

MY FIRST REAL CONTACT WITH GOD

I was tempted to leave out this part, but, to me, this is one of the greatest experiences that I have ever had since I came to know the Lord, and I think by telling this part of my life it might help someone. Now, as you can see from the previous chapters, I had many great experiences that proved to me that God is real, but some of these were through dreams and visions. This one that I am about to tell is real, so much so that even I became amazed at the glory of God.

As a young Christian, I was very easy to get along with, and so it became natural that I ended up having a lot of friends, both male and female. I also made friends quickly, and I was always a true friend. Maybe, as I grew older and acquired a little wisdom, I may have changed somewhat, but I still get along fairly well with almost everyone. For example, I can't remember having any enemies in all my life. If there were any, I was not aware of them. As it turned out, I ended up having a lot of female friends, even though in most of our correspondences we mostly encouraged each other in the Lord.

Every now and then, though, something would happen that let me know that some of these girls would like to take our relationship a bit further, which I was not ready for. I was also afraid that if I committed to one, it might break the others' heart, so I avoided this as much as possible. However, while in the ministry, you can never overlook the fact that one day you will finish school and instead of going back home to mama and daddy, brothers and sisters, you might end up on your own in a strange part of the country or even a strange land, and you will need a companion.

You don't want to go it all alone, so sometimes, as young men living together at Bible school, we talked about things such as this. Even if you didn't talk, you were probably thinking about which girl would make a good wife and help you in your ministry. Sometimes we received visits from some of our elder pastors, some of whom had suffered on the field and others who had good times.

Some of their stories made us fearful because even though we knew that the Lord was with us and that everything would be all right, we would sit and wonder what life would be like out there. Today we would be in high spirits, and tomorrow we would come down to earth again. Most of the ministers' encouragement to us was to try and find a wife before we enter the ministry. They said it was safer for us and our ministry that way.

I didn't think this would be too hard for me, but which of these women would be right for me? Everyone was nice, but everyone is always nice until you marry them. As far as I could remember, I had at least thirteen women to pick from, and this was trouble; it was hard to choose. I was careful not to make commitments to any, nor did I get closer to any one over the others. I did not commit sin with any because I valued my relationship with God; I knew not to place myself in situations that would jeopardize my relationship with God. But what should I do?

After thinking about this for a while and talking it over with my preacher brothers, I knew I had to do something. I took my concern to God; by faith I went to the Lord. I prayed, "Dear Father, I know You care for me, and You want the best for me. Which of these girls should I ask to be my wife?" After praying, I waited for an answer, but God did not answer me.

Instead, the devil said to me, "What is this you are asking the Lord about? God does not answer that kind of prayer." However, I never gave up. I kept praying on this matter, but there was still no answer. I fasted and prayed more, and one day, the Spirit said to me, "None of them." I was not ready for this answer, and I told myself that something was wrong. All of these girls were Christians; we went to church together, worshipped together, and I listened to their testimonies. Surely there had to be some mistake. I prayed again, calling each girl's name to the Lord. Again He said no to all of them. I tried to persuade the Lord that there had to be one girl in this group that was my wife to be, but again He rejected them all.

Soon, it happened that almost every time I prayed this was a part of my prayer, until one night we all got ready for bed. As I dressed for bed and went to lie down, I heard the voice of God call me. The dorm was filled with now sleeping men, but I heard the voice of the Lord, clear and still, calling me, "Curtis."

I had heard this voice before, so I recognized it and answered, "Yes, Lord?"

"Arise and go to that new building on the other side of the campus. I need to talk to you."

Now in Jamaica, our people put fear in the mind of almost every child when we are growing up, and made us afraid of the dark so that when it gets dark, you will hardly find anyone walking alone in the dark.

Almost all children are afraid of ghosts and at night stayed inside where they felt safe from things that wandered in the dark. So, for me to get up and walk in the dark passing by some graves to go to where the Lord sent me was not good.

"Lord," I said, "Why don't You speak to me right here?"

"I need you to spend some time with Me," He said. "Arise and come."

I got up, put on my shoes, opened the door, and stepped outside. Some of the path was lit, but as I turned a corner, passing the burial ground to enter the side to the building to where the stairs led to the upper floor, it was dark and I became very afraid. I would have turned back, but the need to be alone with the Lord pushed me on. I entered the building and started climbing the stairs. Everything around me was so dark I could hardly find my way. I walked to the far side of the building and knelt down. The first thing I said was, "Lord, I am here as You asked, but I am very afraid."

As soon as these words left my mouth, the place lit up with a beautiful glow. Even now I can still remember this light. After this experience, every time I try to explain the glory, I've never been able to really describe it in it fullness. It was like a holy glow that pierced right into my innermost being.

It was a soft light, not as bright as the sun, but much stronger. Yet it did not hurt. I cannot remember anything in all my years that has made me feel the same way I felt that night. I was so comfortable. It was as if I was lying in the clouds. The hard concrete floor I was kneeling on felt like cotton. Then I felt as if I was covered under the great wings of a mighty angel. All my fears went away, and I felt secure and safe. I knew I was in the presence of the Lord.

I was ready to stay there forever. Then, God started to talk to me. He showed me my life, what it would be like, and far away I saw a girl standing alone. He said, "This woman is your wife, and when the time comes she will come to you. You do not have to go looking for her; she is already prepared for you. I am the Lord. I love you with a perfect love. I will never leave you. Only trust in Me." His words were so comforting, I wanted to stay there forever; I did not want this to be over. How beautiful heaven must be! After a while, He said, "I have to go."

"Can I go with You?" I asked.

"No," He said. "You still have much more work to do for Me." Oh, how I wished that it could go on a little longer, but soon the glory lifted and He was gone. With my heart filled with praise, I rose from my knees and walked back to the dorm.

Strangely enough, this time, even though I went back the same way I came before, I had no fear. When I reached the dorm, the place was quiet except for the sound of snoring; everyone was sound asleep. I lay on my bed for a while. How is it that they say no one can see the Lord and live? Then I remembered that I never really saw the Lord; I was only in His presence. My friends, God is real.

The next day was a brighter day. My prayer was answered. I was now fully assured that my life was in the hands of God. I did not have to make many plans for my life, because His will was my command. I tried to share my experience with my fellow students and friends on campus, but some doubted, because many people, even though they have been saved for a long time, had never experienced a close relationship with our Lord. Some that heard my story rejoiced with me. Oh, bless the Lord!

Days, weeks, and months went by, and soon it was one year. We had our final exams, and now we were getting ready for our graduation. I remember I had just one pair of shoes. I had it for more than three years, and it really looked bad. I wore it so much that the heel was lean to one side, and it was bent out of shape. I needed a new pair of shoes for my graduation. Even though I had loved ones in America that I could ask, I did not want to worry them with every need that came up.

I also knew that there were other people who cared about me and who would buy me a pair of shoes if I asked, but I had my pride, and I did not want to look like a beggar. I knew someone who I could go to at any time and He would not get tired of me; His name is Jesus. He had become a very close friend to me; we talked a lot, so, yes, He told me that whatever I needed, just ask Him and He will do it.

So, I went and talked to my Lord about my problem. "Jesus," I prayed. "Graduation is on June 17, and I need a pair of shoes to wear to the ceremony. Please help me." Graduation was one month away, so to ask for what I needed now would give the Lord plenty of time to send me the shoes I asked for. I rose from off my knees, confident that my prayer would be answered because this was not the first time I asked the Lord for something and He granted it. When you want to build your faith, all you have to do is remember the past, when you were in some kind of trouble and the Lord came through for you. This certainly can do something to your faith, and this was what happened to me on that day; my faith was lifted up because of what He had done for me in the past.

As the days passed, all you could hear and see around school were signs of everyone getting ready for graduation. The guys were getting new clothes and new shoes. I wasn't worrying about clothes because I had good clothes, but I need shoes, and although I waited and prayed, still nothing happened. Weeks passed, and still nothing. It was now only fourteen days to graduation. What was I going to do? I started thinking of a way out. I thought about my pastor; I thought about my friends; I thought about my family in America. It seemed as if God had forgotten me; I needed help. I knew that my family in America would help, but it was too late to ask them now. I only had fourteen days to go, and every avenue looked dark. Had God really forgotten me?

In desperation, I went back to pray. I cried out, "Lord, help me!" This time it seemed as if God was nowhere to be found. I got my clothes ready and waited for an answer from God. Instead, Satan came and put some doubt in my mind. "Look," he said. "You are wasting your time praying. God is not hearing you." Fear gripped me, so I went back to pray one more time. I prayed for help from God. With just seven days to go, I had everything ready for graduation except the shoes.

On the Tuesday before graduation, I made up my mind that all hope was gone. I was not going to get a new pair of shoes. I reached under my bed, took out my old shoes, and cleaned it very well to get it ready for graduation. On Wednesday, I received an envelope with a short note which said, "This is to buy your shoes." There was no name on it. The envelope contained the right amount of money for my shoes. I held it up to God and said thank you. I went and bought my shoes. Now, thanks be to God, I was ready for my graduation. Once more, I learned my lesson. Sometimes we need to wait on the Lord; He *is* a present help in the time of trouble.

· · · · ·

After my graduation, I was placed in the district of Hibernia as a full-time pastor. This was easier to do now that I did not have school anymore. Brother Grant was also a great help to me and a great encouragement to the church. We put our all into the work of God, and suddenly life began to be a real test. Here we were, two young men running the church. Now it was obvious to everyone that we were there to stay and not just to start a church and run off, as we learned many had done before, because Hibernia was not one of the best places to start a church.

The church started growing; more mothers, fathers, sons, daughters, young, and old were added to the church daily. Then trouble started. It seemed as if most of the young girls had their eyes on us. We knew better than to let ourselves fall into these temptation, because we were trained for this. We went to this field with our eyes wide open, but still this cost great strain on our ministries. We made sure never to be seen with any of the girls alone, and we made sure that, at all times, we were in the presence of our guide, Brother Griffith. This did not stop the devil from planning against us, though.

After church on Sunday nights we often spent the night with Brother Griffith and then on Monday we would go to our own home. One night, Brother Grant was inside the bedroom, and I was getting my clothes ready for church on Sunday. The kitchen was outside, a little way from the house. I went to the kitchen and started a fire to heat the iron to press my clothes.

The one I was about to use back then was a heavy piece of iron, shaped like the one we have today, with a handle attached. To heat this up so that it could be used to iron the clothes, we made a fire with wood or coal, put the iron on this fire, and wait for it to get hot. When it was hot, we would take it, and clean any black soot from it, so I could press my clothes without soiling them. This was what I was going to do. I left Brother Grant in the house and went out to get the iron. As I walked into the kitchen and reached in the fire for the iron, with a cloth protecting my hand, I felt someone grab my hand and hold me firmly. Turning, I came face-to-face with a woman. She was very strong; her grip was firm. I had seen her attending church, but I could not remember her making any firm commitment. Today, however, she gave me the shock of my life. I never expected this. I stuttered, "What, what are you doing?"

"Tonight is the night, Brother Peart," she said. "Tonight is the night." I knew she did not come to hurt me; she just hoped I would desire her. This time I took some authority and asked, like I didn't know what she was talking about, "Tonight is the night for what?" She did not answer; she just held me more firmly.

"Let me go," I demanded, but she just held tighter. "If you don't let me go, I will burn you with this iron." She took my hand that held the iron and, taking the iron from me, put it down. In all my life, I never knew that a woman could be so strong. She very easily overpowered me.

Then she said, "I want you, and I will have you tonight." This woman was not about to take no for an answer, so we started to struggle, but she was strong; she was getting the better of me. The night was dark, so no one could see us and come to my aid, but still my only chance was to cry out for help.

"Help!" I cried as loud as I could.

Still, she held me firmly. I was hoping my brother in the house would hear me and come to me. "Help," I cried again, and then a young man heard and came running.

"What are you doing with pastor," he said and tried to pull her away from me. She let go of me, and they both started struggling. I saw my chance to escape, and I headed for the house and safety.

I told the people in the house what had happened. They never heard my cries for help.

The next day was Sunday. We went to church and had a good time worshiping our Lord. Monday I went home. It was clear the devil tried to end my ministry, but thank God I overcame that night.

My life changed drastically. I made my abode in Hibernia and soon became a farmer, cultivating things like carrots, cabbage, potatoes, yams, and such. I received a lot of help on my farm and not long after I was having large produce. As I told you earlier, I was a tailor by trade, and it was not long before the district learned this.

First, I started working in the town of Christiana. I did this for about one year, and because I was now getting so much work from the people in Hibernia, I decided to start my own business in Hibernia. So I started seeking for a place and soon found the perfect spot for my shop. I was on my own and was now making clothes for the people in the district. I must confess, I felt perfectly at home with these people. I worked on my trade in the day and had church in the night. Before long, no one was fighting against me. I was fully accepted as one of the people, and everyone showed me love and I loved them.

Since I was new in the district and because I had none of my family around, the church called a meeting and my welfare was discussed such as how I would get my clothes taken care of and how would I get my food. Later, they came up with a place for me to live and a place where my food and clothes would be taken care of. These people were very good. I was told that this place, Hibernia, was one of the worst places to be, but this was one of the best places and best people I ever lived with.

With all of this happening, I never really got rid of the problem with women, being a young man in the district with so many good qualities. I was a pastor almost, and every woman in those days would be happy to be the wife of a pastor. I was also a farmer;

I always had food, so if I had a family, they would not go hungry. Furthermore, I had a trade, which meant that I would always make money. Tailoring was a profitable trade. Finally, I was not from there. Most women dreamed of finding someone who was not from their district. So, I had problem.

It felt good to have the attention of so many women, but after a while it became too much, and it was not good for my image as a pastor. Every day, they would come to my work place; many women went out of their way to buy me gifts; some of them were not even saved, but still they came.

The home where my food and clothes were taken care of was chosen by a vote because, as I learned later, many of the members were willing to take up this task. One woman in particular was a mother and had raised many kids in this district. She had raised all her children and even some who were not hers and was well loved by everyone. She was also one of the most respectful women in the community and had become a member of my church who had proven herself to be a perfect mother and true Christian.

She had a granddaughter, who she appointed to take care of me. At the time, this granddaughter was not saved, but she was very good. She made sure my clothes were always clean and my food was always good. After a while, I wondered if I was becoming a burden, but she said she counted it as a privilege to take care of me. I became very fond of her; she was precious to me.

She cooked my food and washed my clothes, and believe me, she did all this perfectly. However, I was not in love with her. In truth, she was one of the most beautiful girls in the district, and as much as I could see, many young men wanted to befriend her. She would not give her heart to the Lord, however, and I did not see myself marrying an unsaved girl. Besides, of all the girls around, she showed the least interest in me.

One day, Brother Grant and I went out. As we came walking back, two men were before us and, because we were near to them, I could hear one said to the other, "You see those young preachers here? All they're here for is to look at girls." I wanted to go to them and say that's not so, but I left it alone. You see, we tried our best to keep ourselves pure. We knew that we must be careful for the sake of the work. Also, there was now a girl that I was in love with at my home church. We did not propose to each other as yet, but we knew that something was growing.

Our church was very strict, and it was very easy to get in trouble, so we were very careful. We went to the same public school, and I liked her from then. Now, as fate would have it, we ended up in the same church. We were very close; whenever we could, we were together. We were careful not to sit together, but she would sit right behind me and some times, while the service was going on, she would push her foot under my seat and play with my feet, sometimes pulling off my shoes. I slipped it back on, but she would take it off again.

I liked this playing because I loved her. I always thought that one day we would get married, but it was not to be so. She came to me one day and said, "Curtis, I am thinking of going to live in Kingston for a while." I protested strongly, but she said very strongly, "I am going." I got upset. I loved her, and I did not want her to go; I was afraid of losing her. I said, "If you go, we might lose each other." I thought that if she loved me, she would change her mind and stay, but the next thing I knew she was gone. We corresponded back and forth, but I believed she was a disobedient woman because she left when I told her not to. She attended my graduation, and we finally ended it.

Not long after that, one woman in particular, who was saved and who was the daughter of one of the higher-class families in the district began showing a lot of interest in my life. I cannot remember exactly how it happened, but soon we were friends, and I thought that this might be my wife. She brought me home and introduced me to her family, and soon almost everyone knew we were in love.

I spoke to my pastor and told my mother, who was now in America. Blossom was very pretty and loved me with all her heart. My pastor, though not happy with this news, encouraged me to be careful and pray about it. "Don't rush into anything," he said and added, "I had my eyes on another girl who would be good for you."

I wondered who, but he just said, "Don't rush into anything; just pray. You are a pastor, and you are going to need someone good for your wife." I wondered why my pastor was not as pleased as I had expected him to be.

In the meantime, our love seemed to get stronger, and it was not long before we started to touch, kiss, and speak sweet words to each other. She treated me so special, and I sank deeper and deeper into trouble. The Bible says that you don't have to completely do the act of fornication, but the Lord said in Matthew 5:28, "Whosoever looked at a woman to lust after her has already committed the act in his heart," so I knew I was in trouble.

Soon, it was not safe for us to be alone together because it was hard to keep our hands off of each other, and it became hard to keep away from each other. Take warning, you can't play with fire without getting burned. By this, I mean, be careful of the situations you put yourself in. You might end up doing, thinking, and saying things that you never dreamed of. I had the chance to talk to many people, young and old, and most say that they are strong enough to overcome any kind of trial or temptation that may come their way, but it is always better to take warning from one who knows.

Soon, the girl who took care of me gave her heart to the Lord and turned out to be a sincere Christian. She and my girlfriend became best friends. They would go places together, such as conventions, fellowships, camp meetings, and rallies. It seemed as if less attention was being paid to me. We now lived our lives as brother and sister in the Lord. One day, as Blossom and I were talking, she held my hand and said, "Pastor, I love you and hope that one day I will be your wife, but if anything happens to me and we don't get married, promise me that you will make Collette your wife."

I snapped at her, "What are you saying, girl?"

"No," she said, "but anything can happen." We did not talk about this anymore. Everything seemed to be working out fairly well. Now that Collette was saved, I felt more comfortable around her. We became good friends. Then, something strange began to happen; it seemed as if I had known this girl all my life, and one day, the voice of God spoke to me, saying, "This woman is going to be your wife. She is the one I told you about."

I was not ready for this; I just shook it off. I already found one girl and proposed to her; no one can love two women at the same time, at least not me. I did not give it any further thought. However, whenever my pastor or any other preacher would come and pay a visit, they would stay at Mother Sue's home, and Collette would be the cook.

One day, my pastor looked me in the eyes and said, "There goes your wife. You are looking at the wrong girl." I just smiled. I knew I was already sold out, mind and soul, to my girlfriend, so whenever I looked at Collette, I made sure I had no such thought in my head. All these women loved God, and we loved to worship together; we all acted like brothers and sisters in the Lord.

HOW I FOUND MY WIFE

I thought I found the right girl who could be my wife. She was loving and kind and seemed to get along with everyone. I had no intention to look anywhere else because, as far as I could see, this girl was everything I dreamed of. I loved a beautiful girl. I needed someone to love me, and she said she did. I wasn't a wild man, so I was not out there seeking as many girls as I could get. I had seen too many men do that.

If we found problems in each other, we talked about it, and this helped us to know each other better. I soon found that it was much better to act natural, because when you are trying so hard to be perfect there are more chances for slipping up. It is much better for you to be natural so that your lover will see the real you and make a clear decision on whether or not they want to marry *you* and not the person you were pretending to be. This is a very great concern, since the plan of God is that when two people find each other and finally get married, they should stay married forever.

This is one very important question that was put to me some time ago. "Pastor, what is marriage?" Marriage, from my point of view, is when two persons are joined together and become one. To many, this may seem to be a mystery, but it is all in God's great plan. The Bible says, "For this cause shall a man leave his mother and father and cleave unto his wife and they shall be one flesh."

This is a sign of God's plan for us, His church. The church is called the bride of Christ, and one day Christ, who is the Bridegroom, will come for His bride to take us to His home, and we shall be married to Him. This is why every marriage should be good, because it is supposed to be an example of God's love for us and our love for Him. So, I believe that every man who treats his wife badly and every woman who treats her husband badly is a bad example of what or who God is and by so doing is sending a bad message to the world. Such husbands and wives need to repent and change.

One day, my ex-girlfriend Blossom came to me and said, "Curtis, my family in the United States is sending for me, and I will be leaving for the States in a month's time." This was disappointing news to me, but what could I do? She had to go. She assured me that she would always be true to me and would seek to stay in the will of God. I had no reason to doubt her word; after all, she had always been faithful. I remained faithful, doing the Lord's work and knowing that I had someone in America who loved me. We kept on corresponding back and forth, but God, my God, never makes mistakes. The Bible says, "The ways of a good man are orders by the Lord." This means that God knows what's good for you, and He will do it for you if you just let Him.

As for my bride-to-be, she seemed to be doing well. She was now in college pursuing a career. I felt so proud of her; she was always a bright girl so being in college was okay. Then, to my surprise, after about six months I received a letter from her saying "Curtis, now that I am in college, I need to break off this friendship for a while." I did not expect this, but I could understand.

She wanted to concentrate on her studies, and having me on her mind was hindering her. I believed this was the reason until I read the other lines that followed. This hit me like a bomb. She said "Now that I have done some studies, I have come to see that there is no God. Pastor, I want you to know that there is no God." You know some people study and learn until they become fools. The Bible says in Psalms 14:1 and 53: 1 that "The fool said in his heart there is no God." I could not believe it!

This was a girl who loved the Lord. Oh, how soon she turned from Him. Without waiting, I took pen and paper and wrote, "Well, my dear, I am so sorry, but you know that I am a Christian and I shall always believe that there is a God. I would never in my wildest dream marry a woman who does not believe in God. Also, I can see that you don't want to go on with this relationship, so I am now ready to call an end to this relationship." I decided then that I would not seek to start another relationship with any other woman because it had been proven that I was a bad judge of character.

Now, as I said before, Collette continued to be very helpful to me, washing my clothes and cooking my food. She was a wonderful cook and still is to this day. Now that she was saved, she was now fully dedicated to her Lord and church, even though the church had many young people, but I could see that serving the Lord was now her greatest interest.

I settled myself into my pastoral work and my job as a tailor, and God blessed me. Collette kept on doing what she had to do for me. She was very kind and loving and worked without receiving a reward. Then one day, while praying, the Lord revealed to me that Collette was going to be my wife. As you may remember, this was the second time that God said this to me. He even went further and said, "I have prepared her for you. Have no fear."

However, I still made no move toward her. Then, my pastor came and told me, "This girl will make you a very good wife." Even the man in whose house I stayed sat me down and showed me all the reasons why he saw this girl was the girl for me. Finally I turned my eyes to look her over, studying her movements, the company she kept, the way she cared for me, and things like that.

To tell the truth, I did not have anything against her, but in my eyes she seemed a little too popular. I had no intention of getting myself involved with a woman such as this. Right now, you might find it hard to understand what I am talking about. Of all the girls in the district, she was the best looking, both in figure and looks; she was one that any man would desire to be with.

On the other hand, I was not too handsome, so you can see my hesitation. However, everything was now pointing toward her. I cannot remember everything that led up to me posing the question to her, but I remember she did not delay to say "yes," so from there on, I spent some time getting to know her.

After courting for a month, I really started to fall in love with this woman. This love was different from all the others; this was not a love at first sight, but I grew to love her. We talked a lot, and soon I was able to learn that this girl was special. I had misjudged. She, unlike many other girls, had vowed to save her love and body for her husband. I learned from her that she watched how some men treated woman, and she had determined from a child that she would not make the same mistake, and she kept her purity. The more I learned about her, the more I grew to love her.

Soon, I knew what I had to do. I went and talked to my pastor. Next, I sent and told my mother and father who were in the United States. Then came the hard part; I had to talk to her family. I called for a meeting, and Collette's father, grandmother, and some of her aunts all gathered to hear what I had to say. This turned out to be one of the hardest things I had ever had to do.

I entered the room where everyone had gathered, and they called Collette. According to their actions, it appeared as if everyone knew why I was there. This made it even harder for me. What if, after I asked for her hand in marriage, they said no? I could just see myself leaving with my head hung low. Collette entered and stared at me. So I looked around the room. Some heads were hung down, and some eyes were staring right at me. After what seemed to be a long period of silence, the father spoke up, "Well, Brother Peart. We are all here as you asked. What is it?"

It was now or never; I had to be brave.

"Well," I began, stuttering. "I am in love with Collette, a-and…I am he-ere to as…k her hand…in marriage." There was a period of silence in the room.

Then her father said, "Let us hear from Collette."

So, the grandmother asked Collette, "You heard what the pastor said. What do you say?" I thought she may not answer, but I was surprised when she replied, "Yes, I do love and want to marry him." I suddenly felt relieved. Yes, it's true; she really loved me. I waited for the verdict.

The father spoke up. "Well," he said, "if you are both in love, we can do nothing but say yes." Everyone agreed. The father turned to me and said, "Thank you, Brother Peart, for being so honest; you both could have gone behind our back and done funny things, but you came to us." Again, everyone agreed.

So now it was out; everyone soon knew that I found the woman who would be my wife. I knew that this was love because of the stumping and fluttering of my heart when I saw her, but a man must be a man; it was best not to let her know what was happening. I had learned that a man must not really show his real feelings, as this was a sign of weakness, but now I say this is not true; it's best to let someone know exactly how you feel. There is nothing wrong with showing that you are human and have feelings. Every day I found myself falling more and more in love with Collette. It even got to the point where, when I did not see her for a time, I longed to see her; my heart would long for her, and my hands longed to hold her. This was not good; we had to keep away from each other, or so I thought. I had to do this for the Gospel's sake. This proved to be hard, not because of the flesh but because of the many eyes that were watching. Something had to be done quickly.

Well, I knew that I found the right girl, or rather, that God had provided the right girl to be my wife, and so I introduced her to the rest of my relatives. She met my aunties, and they all loved her and welcomed her with opened arms. I took her to meet with my uncles, and they were so excited; some shook her hand, some hugged her, some kissed her, but all welcomed her to the family. She was also introduced to my brothers and sisters, who welcomed her and showed their love. I was glad that my family approved of her.

With all this behind me, it was time to move on; we had a wedding to plan, so we went and met with our pastor. So Pastor Lodge helped to instruct us and even helped us set a date for the wedding. My pastor was a good man, one of the greatest men I ever met. With a date in mind, both families were notified, and that was all we had to do. Pastor decided that we should not wait too long; he did not say it, but knowing the man I knew, he wanted this over with as fast as possible so as to prevent us from committing fornication. So, we only had three months to prepare for the wedding. I told my mother and the family who were now in America the plans and the date of the wedding, and they appointed one of my uncles to be in charge of the affairs. From then on, everything was taken out of my hands, and the family did everything.

On our wedding day, I went to church fifteen minutes before the ceremony was scheduled to begin. All was set, and I settled down to wait with my best man by my side, giving words of encouragement because I was nervous. Oh, how I wanted this to be over with! I stood up; I sat down again and waited, every now and again looking toward the door, hoping to see my bride. Ten minutes passed, and then half an hour passed. What was going on? I thought to myself, *I thought this girl wanted to get married. Where is she?*

My best man saw that I was getting impatient and again tried to comfort me. "Don't worry," he said. "That's how the ladies do it. They like to let the man wait." I looked at him and smiled. All the guests were there, but there was no bride. Suddenly a thought flashed in my mind; I wondered if she had changed her mind. Would she do this to me?

I heard stories of things like this happening, husbands waiting in chapel for their brides, but they never show up. I just hoped this was not happening to me. Just then, the marriage officer came and gave me some words of comfort, almost the same thing my best man said before. He said, "Don't worry. She will be here. Of all the weddings I performed, the bride was never early." This made me feel better, so I settled down and waited. Not very long after, someone said, "The bride is here."

I stood and took my place at the altar with my best man. I looked toward the door, not knowing what to expect. My heart leaped; she was now at the door. I had known this woman for a long time, and I was used to seeing her dressed up, but today she looked exceptional. She looked like a doll. As she walked gracefully into the church hall, I walked to meet her. I saluted her and took her right hand into mine. Together we walked to the altar where the minister was waiting. In my mind I said, "Thank you, Lord, for making this woman for me."

"Curtis," the minister said, "will you have this woman to be your wedded wife, to have and to hold from this day forward, to love and to cherish, in sickness or in health, for better or for worst, until death you do part?" I looked at her standing like an angel by my side, and then I looked at the minister and said, "I will." The guests cheered.

Then he said, "Collette, look at this man standing beside you and answer me this question." She looked at me very lovingly and then back at the minister. The minister asked her, "Collette, will you have this man to be your wedded husband, to live together after God's holy ordinances, will you love honor and keep him, in sickness or in health, forsaking all others, keep thee only unto him, as long as you shall live?" She said, "I will."

He then counseled us to be always good to each other and to be each other's best friend. Then, he asked for the ring, blessed it, and gave it to me to place on her finger. Then he prayed for us, and pronounced us man and wife, saying "Who God join together, let no man put asunder."

Everyone came running to us to congratulate us and wish us much blessing and health. We thanked everyone for coming and walked out of the church, hand in hand, to the car that was waiting, and away we went. The driver took us touring for a while and then to my grandparents home, where the reception was being held.

As the car drove up to the house, we saw everyone waiting. Some were busy eating. A procession led us inside the house, which was well decorated. It was the first time I had a chance to see this, because every time I tried to get a peak at what they were doing and to see if there was anything I could do to help, they would refuse my help and my money; they did it all by themselves. I was pleased with how well they decorated the place. Everyone was happy; there was plenty of food and drinks, and everyone had a good time. They toasted and drank, danced and laughed. The funny thing was, though, that we didn't get any food!

The reception lasted until nightfall, and when it was all over there was nothing left for us to eat, so we had to go to our place hungry while everyone was full. For some strange reason, they forgot to save food for us. This was something I never forgot about our wedding day; they sent us home with some wedding cake and a gallon of wine.

My pastor helped us to find a place that I rented and moved into with my new wife. Yes, I was now a married man, and my wife a married woman. It was very awkward moving into my own apartment with a woman. The landlord, knowing that we just got married, came and congratulated us, then opened our room and sent us to bed. This was surely strange; my wife and I sat for long time talking of the day's event; none of us seemed ready to go to bed, even though we were tired; going to bed together was indeed a strange feeling.

In the morning, neither of us wanted to go out. How could we look these people in the eye, seeing that we slept together? They might ask us questions we didn't care to answer. We woke up and sat in our room; no, we would not face them. After a while, the landlord's wife knocked on our door. She knew that we had been up for a long time, because she must have heard us talking.

"Pastor," she called, "I left some breakfast in the kitchen. I have to go to the town, and my husband went to work."

I answered, "Okay," feeling happy that at least I did not have to face them yet. Then she said, "Did you have a good sleep last night?"

"Yes," I answered.

"Good, then see you later."

"Okay." Now that the way was clear, we came out of our room into the bright sunshine and thanked God for another day.

Well, after my wedding, I learned that I was not going to be at Hibernia anymore. The reason was not fully explained to us, but one day I received news from the headquarters that we would be going to another parish to pastor another church, and they would send a new pastor to Hibernia to take my place. I reasoned it out for myself; I believed that because I was married to someone from Hibernia, they decided that it was best I didn't stay. So we were sent to a place called Crescent in the parish of St. Mary. The church was small and had its own parsonage on the property.

We were taken there by our superintendent. He helped us to move all our things to this new place. He took us to the place and said good-bye. Then, before driving off, he said, "If you need anything, just speak to the neighbor next door." I could not believe it; they took us from our district were we knew everyone and everyone knew us and placed in a strange place and left us without food or money.

"Wait," I said to the overseer, "let me see who is next door and if it's someone we can depend on to supply our needs." When I got there, I was surprised to see some people who, by their appearances, were not even saved. I introduced myself as the new pastor who came to take over, but they did not show much interest. I knew we were in trouble. I ran back to the overseer and said, "I don't see anyone of interest there, so you can't leave us like this, with not even food to start with." So, he reached into his pocket and gave me some money and said, "Try it out here for a time, see if you like it; you might."

That day, my wife and I got busy and started to fix up the place. The rooms were big, so we planned to make the best of what we had. After all, this was going to be our new home for only God knew how long. My wife was very good; in little to no time she made the house look and feel like a home. I went to the little shop down the hill, not far away, and got something to cook, and she got dinner ready.

It was not long that the place was filled with people of the church. They wanted to see what their new pastor looked like. I never had to ask; I knew that was why many of them came. They greeted us and welcomed us to the place and wished that we would stay for a long time; some even brought us some food. It seemed that things would not be as bad as it first seemed.

The next day, two men of the village came to show us around and introduce us to some of the villagers. The place was very fruitful, and the rivers were full of fishes and other different kinds of creatures. As we met everyone, they seemed to be friendly and also happy to have us come to minister to them. Sunday turned out to be really good; almost all the district came out to see who the new pastor was and to hear him preach. I had no problem with this, because this was a very good opportunity to meet everyone.

After church, I met everyone and even learned a few names. I really felt welcomed that day. Then someone asked if I needed anything. I requested jelly coconut, so we were taken to a coconut tree. Everyone said I would be unable to drink two, because the coconuts were so big. I told them I would be able to have more than two, so, to prove me wrong, they took me to a tree that they knew had fruits with a lot of water that I would be unable to manage.

To their surprise, I had three and also ate all of the jelly. In Manchester we did not have many coconut trees; therefore, the few people who had these trees on their properties protected them with their life. We seldom ate jelly coconuts, and when we did, we had to buy them. So, just imagine coming to another parish, St. Mary, where every place you looked there were coconut trees. Eventually, though, I did not care much for coconuts anymore, even though they were good for me.

But let's look at this: Do you know what a jelly coconut looks like. How does the water get into this nut? Don't you think there is a God somewhere?

WE COME UPON HARD TIMES IN THE NEW FIELD

Well, it was not long before we learned that our new field was a poor area, and most people depended on their farms and any little odd jobs they could find. Soon, life became really hard for us; there were a lot of fruits around, but who can live on fruits alone? At least we had food were we came from in Manchester.

I also noticed that the boring life in this place was having a toll on my wife, even though she tried not to show it; she tried to be content with the little we had. We often waited longingly for letters from our relatives in America, because they always sent some money in it, but these only came sometimes. We knew what it meant to suffer on the field; many nights, my wife and I went to bed hungry, and after a while she started to make it known to me that she was unhappy with this place I chose to take her.

To her, this was not a joke anymore. It did not take me long to learn that if your wife is not happy, you will have trouble, so after a while our happy married life changed, and almost every day we argued. She was unhappy in this place, but she failed to tell me.

I couldn't see what her problem was; maybe if she had said to me "I hate this place; I want to go," then I would have taken her somewhere else, but she did not want to stand as a hindrance in my ministry and so kept on sacrificing her happiness. I saw from her actions that she was not happy.

One day, she told me she longed to see her family and wished to go pay them a visit. Hoping that this would help to cheer her up, I agreed and sent her to see them. I waited for her to return, but she ended up staying longer than we had planned. Then, one day, I received a letter from her saying, "I am not coming back."

For a month, I stayed alone and served the church, hoping that she would soon miss me and come home, but two more weeks passed, and she seemed to be getting comfortable away from me. So I packed my bag and went for her. She did not refuse; she just packed and came back with me. Things didn't change much after that, but she never tried to leave again; she just stayed and tried to please me. She was really sent by the Lord, and I was so very happy for her.

Things were not all bad; we had some good times, bathing in the river, fishing, and going for long rides on my bicycle. We were not living far from the sea, so we spent a lot of our time on the beach. We had long walks in the wood, sightseeing, and sometimes we even went to the town. We enjoyed walking hand in hand as we often did on our strolls.

Even though all this was good, I longed to give my wife the good things she should have in life, because this was a part of my duty as a husband. She had, to the best of her ability, done her part, and now I needed to fulfill her dream, but how could I do this? The church could not give me a salary, because most Sundays we never collected much for offering or tithes. I would work if I could find a job, but there were no jobs in this area. If it was up to me, I would pack and leave, because we could go back home to our parish where I knew things would be better, but I never tried to do things on my own. I knew by experience to always wait on the Lord to give the okay, and until now He had not given the okay so we stayed and try to make the best of it.

GOD CHOSE A WIDOW TO TAKE CARE OF US

One Saturday, as we sat on a bench in the yard under a tree, we saw a little boy coming up the hill with a basket on his head. We had nothing to eat all day but some mangos. The little boy entered the yard, came up to us, and said, "Pastor, Grandma sent this for you." We took the basket off his head and carried it into the house. My wife began to take the things out and put it on the table. To our surprise, everything we needed and more was there. God had come through for us again. We said thanks to the child for carrying the things to us and told him to say thanks to his grandmother.

Sunday after church, my wife and I walked over to his grandmother to say thank you and to let her know how much what she had sent was well appreciated. This was when she explained to us that she hoped she could have done more.

She said, "Pastor, I bought myself a basket with two sides and from this day, onward every day that I go to the market to do my shopping, everything I buy for myself I will also buy for you." Her name was Miss Lulleater Paisley; with this lady and the help from my relatives from America, our life made a change for the better.

Our lives went through some drastic changes. My wife became pregnant, and we had a son we named Richard St. Albin Peart. This brought much happiness to the family. I did not have to do much; the ladies of the church came every day and left late at night to take care of my wife and our son until she was strong enough to take over and even after that they still came.

The Lord was very good to us, and I soon became a very popular pastor in the district. I was called upon many times to perform duties like praying in school, officiating weddings, funeral, and christening of babies, home visits, and various kinds of counseling. While on this subject, I can remember that there was this young girl in this district. She was very beautiful and was more attractive that other girls around. All the young men longed to be her friend. My home was near the road that goes through the district, so I could see everyone that passed by. Sometimes I would call them over and talk to them about giving their lives over to Christ.

This girl was one of them that I spoke to every chance I got. One day, as I pleaded with her, she replied, "Pastor, one day I will give up and serve the Lord, but I am too young to do that now. Maybe one day when I am much older." I explained to her that the Bible said, "Behold today is the day of salvation, and if you hear His voice harden not your heart." But she refused, saying, "I am young; I have time." After that day, she avoided me as much as possible.

One day, we noticed something strange: No matter how hot the time was, this girl wore a long-sleeved sweater. Everyone started wondering why. Some speculated that maybe she was pregnant and was using the coat to hide her stomach. Months passed, and then we didn't see her again on the street. Soon we received news that she was sick at home with some strange form of ailment.

They took her to many doctors and hospitals, but there was no cure. In fact, they could not tell what this sickness was. Something appeared on her hand like a scab, and it had spread all over her body; the more they tried to treat it, the more it would spread. Soon, it covered her whole body. I was called to give a house visit. When I got into the house, the girl wouldn't let me look on her. She was covered from head to feet with a white sheet. "Enid," I said, "this is Pastor."

From under the cover she said, "Yes, Pastor."

"Some time ago, I asked you if you would like to accept the Lord as your Savior, and you said no. Would you like to give your heart to Him now?"

"Yes, Pastor."

I spoke to her about giving up to the Lord and then I prayed for her and asked her, "Have you now fully given up to the Lord?"

"Yes, Pastor," she said. I said good-bye and left. As soon as I stepped into my house, I received news that she died. I never forgot this young girl. May this be a warning to all that even though you might feel good and strong today, no man knows what tomorrow holds. Listen to this warning and make it right with God before it is too late.

While living in St. Mary, I remember having a near-death experience that helped affirm the answer to the question: is God real or what? While living in this district, we had to have some way of getting around. You see, everywhere we had to go was far away, so it was important to have some form of transportation. Now all I could afford was a bicycle. This became our form of transportation, and I was happy for it. I used it to go almost everywhere, often carrying my wife on the crossbars.

At this time, the main roads were paved, but the smaller roads—like the one we took home—were rough and very steep. One day while riding down this hill, as I had done so many times before, I was going down too fast, so the wheel kept bouncing up and down. Suddenly, my front wheel flew off and I went flying though the air.

I went over the handle bar, and I fell on my stomach, hitting my face on the ground. I tried to get up but found that it was hard to do with no one there to help me. I rolled to one side and then, with much effort, I sat up, dazed, cut, and bruised all over. Coming to my senses, I looked around and then, although hurting, gave praises to God for saving my life because, no less than six inches from where my head hit the ground was a big rock. If my head had hit this rock, I would have died. Praise God! One more time He was watching over me. I got up and scrambled back up the hill, back to my home. There my wife helped me. She washed and dressed my wounds and in two weeks, except for the marks on my body, I was as good as new. I repaired my bike and was back on the road again.

Another day, I left the house to go to the shopping area to get something for my wife. When I got to the store, my money was one dollar short. I thought about what to do. Should I ask someone for a dollar or go back home and wait until I had the full amount of money? Because I knew I had taken all we had as money and went to the store, my mind would not allow me to ask any one for help. So I finally decided to go back home and come back when I have the money. I knew my wife would be disappointed; she was not well and needed this medicine.

As I walked home, pushing my bicycle because I was not in the mood to ride up the hill to my home, I started talking with my Lord. In this brief moment, I took time to evaluate my life and my stand with God. It occurred to me that I had not asked the Lord for what I needed; all I needed was a dollar. Why didn't I ask?

I thought of all the possible ways I could raise a dollar but never thought of asking God. It was just as if I was snapped back into my senses. I can still remember that day as if it were today. The wind was blowing; the leaves were flying all over the path. I had now reached to where bamboo trees hung over the path. On the hottest of days, this spot was cool. Just over the left side was a gully with a river. I can still hear the sound of the river as the water ran over and along the stones.

I stopped, looked up to the sky, and spoke to God. "Daddy," I said, "please, I am asking You for a dollar." I started walking again pushing my bike, and as I looked on the ground before me, there was a dollar on the ground. I ran to get it; I was so happy to see it and was afraid that the wind would blow it away since the leaves were blowing all around it. Then, I heard the voice of the Lord say, "You don't have to run and grab it; you asked for it so I gave it. I am holding it for you; the wind cannot blow it away." So I calmed down and walked normally and picked it up. I said, "Thank You, Lord," and returned to get what I needed. Is God real or what?

We continued living in Crescent, where we gained much experience. My wife started an infant school and also offered after school programs. This offered much-needed help for some of the children, and many people welcomed this. It did not bring in much income, however, because most of the people could not pay; this was mostly a volunteer service.

Then, came the day that, because of the circumstances, we decided it was time to go. We packed and were off the very next day. We went back to our home, Manchester, where we rented an apartment and settled down. We started to attend our old church, but, before long we were offered another church to pastor. This church was in a district called Moravia.

Before we got there, we received so much bad news about this place—about how the people of this church were difficult to lead. This was not good news, as we were just leaving a church that would not take instruction and so many of the church members failed to live right. Were we going to go through the same thing again? My pastor confirmed that the news about our new church was true but said, "All you do, Pastor Peart, is just preach the Word. Someone will want to hear it. The Bible says to us 'preach the word, in season and out of season.' This means, brother, when they want to hear it and when they don't want to."

Now, the church in Moravia was not very far from where we now lived, and it was said that pastors who go there never stayed for long because the people in this church had "bad ways." However, while I worried about this matter, about whether it was a good idea to go to this place, I had a vision that soon confirmed that this was where the Lord wanted me to go, so it was now settled in my mind. I would go and be a pastor to these people. My pastor was the overseer for this church, and he was the one who introduced my wife and me to the people.

Many of these people were older and I was pretty young, so they were puzzled. I think this was the first time they were offered such a young pastor. I was now twenty-three years old and my wife was seven months younger than I was. After I had been with them for a while, they testified to me of what they were thinking when I first came. Many elder pastors had come and had to leave, so here I was, a young man in many minds, and they were wondering if I could manage.

Well, in my mind, this new church seemed to be ideal for my wife and I, and we were up to the challenge. Besides, there were several benefits for being the pastor of this church: It was located about ten miles from where we lived; we would be close to both our families, about fifteen miles from my wife's relatives, and about twelve miles from mine.

We would be back in the area where we were both born and raised; and the young people of this church seemed happy to have a young pastor for a change. So, we accepted the call to serve, and the next Sunday I took over as pastor for the church in Moravia. The church had about thirty-five members, and on my first Sunday they all came to church. We had a very good service because I was ready to prove that I was well able to carry on this church.

After pastoring for about two months, though, I discovered some problems in the church. For one, some of these people only wanted to be members of a church, but, as far as living holy, this was not their intention. I found that they did not want me to preach against sin, but I was determined to do just that. So, after a few weeks, less and less people attended my services. I started visiting some homes to see if I could find out what was wrong. I soon discovered from some that my sermons were too much for them, and so they stayed away.

I decided that, even though I may be losing members, I would not "water down" the gospel, because there were a chosen few who wanted me to make sure they were ready for heaven. In the following weeks, I called the faithful to fasting and prayer and, after about two weeks, we had a revival. Many people became saved. We started having baptism, and the power of God was revealed in the place. Some of those who went away came back to church.

I often walked to church because there was no transportation going there. Sometimes I would spend the night near the church so that I could be there for Sunday school in the morning. My wife was often with me. This is another reason why, no matter what happens in my life, my wife is to be commended, because through rain and sunshine she was with me all the way. Soon she became pregnant again and gave birth to a lovely baby girl. She was so lovely, we decided to name her Lavinia and nicknamed her Lovie.

The Lord eventually blessed me with another bicycle, which was a great help to me. One day, as I pushed my bicycle to church because the hill was too steep to ride up, I approached a man sitting on the street-side. I said good day to him, and he replied, "Today you are pushing a bicycle, but a few days from now you will be driving your car over this hill." He said this mockingly, but his words came through, because a few days later I was able to buy a car. Now, I didn't have to walk or ride a bicycle to church; I could drive.

The Lord started adding to the church daily, and the saints were restored. After a year, I was able to confess that this was one of the best churches I had ever pastored. The Christians were loving and considerate and very well consecrated; I hardly had any trouble with this church. All the other ministers who warned me that I was going to have a hard time with this church were surprised at the church.

I stayed as pastor for this church for about three years and experienced good times and bad, but the good far outweighed the bad. I can remember one night after church when we got into the car and headed home. Halfway home, the car broke down. My wife, who was then pregnant with our third child, had to help me push the car. This was hard because we had to push it over a hill. We soon got help from others, and as soon as we got home we had to take her to the hospital. She gave birth to another baby girl. We called her Rowena. Now it was my wife, our three kids, and I in the car going to church and any other place we had to go.

Although I now had a family to support, I never let up on the work of God and still had a caring heart for those in need. I remember one evening, my wife asked me to go out and get sugar and bread. As I was going to the store, I passed a poor beggar along the way. He looked so rejected and lonely.

When I was coming back from the store, he was still sitting there on the sidewalk. I could not pass him; my heart went out to him, and I walked over to him and asked, "Sir, are you hungry?" He looked up at me and said, "Yes." I opened the bread, broke it in half, and gave one half to him. He said thanks and started eating. I immediately felt a happy feeling, knowing I was able to provide food for him. I went home and told my wife what had happened. She was not too happy with my action, but she soon forgave me.

Life was hard, but it was much better than it was in St. Mary. Many things in my life also changed. Sometimes, I used my car as a taxi. This helped to bring some needed funds into our life. The car got better with age, which was a blessing of God because other people had this same model car and even younger, and they had so much trouble. But my car just kept on going and going. Thanks be to God for favor.

Things began to get easier for the family, as God really blessed me. I learned to love the people of my church, and they loved me, so we stayed and served in this church, and soon I was asked to help out in another church in the district of Burn-Cider in the parish of Clarendon. So, every other Sunday, I would travel to this church. This was a lot of work, but someone had to do it and I was the one chosen. So now I was serving two churches, but I was encouraged because the people of the second church were loving, and they welcomed me.

I served these two churches until my family and I were invited to migrate to America. This was so hard to do since we had fallen in love with these people. However, for about seven years I had been granted the opportunity to travel, but I never could. My life had been sold out to the Lord, and I was not my own; I had to wait for the word from the Lord.

This was what happened while in the service of the Lord in Jamaica: Even though the opportunity came over and over again, I had to wait until the Lord said I could go. Since He never said go, I stayed put. Then one day, the Lord spoke to me. "You can go now. You will see that because you have been faithful, I now make the way easy for you."

And it was, because while in Jamaica, I had seen many who desired to travel to another country, even for a visit, but had been turned down by the immigration over and over again. However, when I got the word go from the Lord, I wrote to my family in America and said I was now ready to come, and in no time my wife, my three children, and I received our papers and were ready for travel.

There is a song that we often sang in our churches that goes like this, "They that wait upon the Lord, shall renew their strength; they shall mount up with wings as eagles; they shall run and not be weary, they shall walk and not faint; teach me, Lord; teach me, Lord how to wait." Oh, yes; I waited, and when the

Lord was ready, all went well. What about you? Have you yet learned to wait on the Lord?

It was now the month of February in 1982. I was sure that I would be leaving for the United States of America. The time of our departure was set; I had to leave the eighteenth of April 1982. I informed the churches of my plans and sent a notice of resignation to my headquarters.

One week before my departure, the main church in Manchester planned a farewell for us, and that Friday night many people came out to bid us good-bye. I can still remember how there was a feeling of happiness and sadness. There was laughing and crying, singing and praying, recalling of memories and hugging, eating and drinking. It was something I will never forget.

I remember one elderly man stood up and spoke. He said, "Brother Peart, you have been faithful in your service for the Lord. Now you are leaving for America. In my many years of serving the Lord I have seen and heard of many Christians who, upon reaching this strange land called America put down the Lord and take up the world. Pastor, we may never meet again in this life here on earth, but I want you to promise me that you will be faithful to your call."

I bow my head and prayed, "Lord, help me to be faithful."

After this service was over, with only one week to go, we took the time to prepare the final touches and went around and said our final good-byes. We were scheduled to leave on that Wednesday at two o'clock in the afternoon. We did our final service on Sunday and learned that our church had chartered a bus and was coming to the airport to see us off.

Although I was happy about this, I would have preferred if they did not. My family and I were already having a very hard time leaving, and we knew that there would be more crying and sad good-byes. I did not want this, so we left early for the airport and, even after we checked in, the bus with our church family still had not arrived. However, as I walked toward the airplane, I heard our names. Someone was shouting out my name.

Looking back, I saw my church brethren all waving and throwing kisses at us. As I lay my left hand on the rail of the steps that lead up into the plane (my family had gone before me), I bowed my head and prayed, "Lord, if You see that I will go to America and fail you, please don't let me leave here."

Others behind me wanted to climb aboard, so I stepped out of their way and continued my talk with God. "Father, I promise to be faithful always with Your help. Amen." I went up to the top of the stairs, where my family waited for me. We stopped once more and waved our last good-bye. We boarded the plane and sat down. This was our first time on an airplane. We were seated close together. We took a moment to look around us and were excited. Surely God was good. Imagine! This plane would soon be lifting off and would be taking 250 people to another land. God is good, giving man the knowledge to build something like this.

On our arrival in United States, we disembarked at the JFK airport and found a group of friends and family waiting to receive us. It was April, but it was still cold, especially for us who were just coming from the Caribbean and had never experienced this cold. There was also some snow on the ground, and this was interesting since that was the first time we had ever seen this white stuff. Our relatives brought us coats, and we put them on, also something new for us because, even though we wore coats in Jamaica, they were never so thick and heavy. As we walked to the car, we thanked God for these coats.

So, my family and I finally settled down, ready to start a new life in this great country of America. I missed my country and the people I left behind, but that's life. I had to move on. I started attending the New Testament Church of God, because that was where my family went. Going to church was a very important part of my life, and I find that even now, when I go on vacation to other countries, on Sundays I have to find a church to attend or I feel like a part of my life has gone unfulfilled.

After about a month, I got a job. This job was waiting for me even before I entered this country. As I said in an earlier chapter, I went into the security field and worked at an apartment complex called Tracy Towers. The job was okay and paid well, even though it was not permanent. At the time, I was working as a standby security guard. Our job was to make sure that the place stayed secure for the safety of the tenants. I was glad I had this job, because I had a family to support, even though I was never in want, because the family stood by us and made sure we had everything we needed and more.

After about a year on this job, I found that all of my coworkers respected me. They knew that I was a Christian and, even though I never asked for it, my life demanded it; everyone, even the manager in the head department, respected me. They were careful of the things they did and said around me, and I respected them for this. So I had no reason to want to leave this job; I loved my job and hoped one day to work there permanently.

Then, about two months later, I was employed permanently. I began to receive visits from the Holy Spirit; sometimes while sitting at my desk, He would come upon me, covering me, which led me to worship. I didn't really want this to happen because I was posted in an open hall and hundreds of people passed my desk daily. A part of my job was to find out from visitors where in the building they were going and record their names as well as the time they came in and went out. This way you know who comes and goes.

Just imagine the Holy Spirit coming upon me as I was doing this; I would look like insane. However, for some reason, even though I often fought hard to prevent this from happening, I still would "get in the Spirit." I didn't get outrageous and carry on foolishly, but yes, I felt the power of God all over me.

Then one day, the Lord spoke to me. He said, "Remember how you promised to continue My work wherever you go?"

"Yes," I said.

"Well, it's time."

"Yes, Lord," I said. "Lead and I will follow." This would happen day after day, but as soon as the power eased off, I went back to my normal self. I thought of my good job and the money I was making; I thought of my family that I had to support. I remembered the many years of suffering on the Lord's mission. Now that I had a chance to make it, how could I give this all up? This happened over and over again.

One day on the job, I had another experience with the Holy Spirit. This time, He came on me so strongly that I felt like crying out, but I controlled myself and moved away from my desk and to a hidden spot in the building. There we (God and I) had a talk. I made reasonable excuses that I was sure God would understand, but then He asked, "Who gave you this job?"

"You, Lord," I replied.

"Who made your mouth?"

"You, Lord."

"Who made your feet, your hands, your ears, and eyes?"

"You, Lord."

"Now remember, I gave it and I have the power to take it away." My many excuses were knocked out of me like the wind, and I stood helpless before God. This part I know you will find hard to believe, but as I spoke, I stood in the presence of the Holy God, and suddenly I felt the powerful hand of God lift me off the ground. I felt very little and insignificant in the presence of God. After a little while, it was all over, although the feeling of being in the glory of His presence, the feeling to worship never left me. I had once again said yes to God; I had to fulfill His will in my life. I knew I could not keep making these excuses.

I thought over these things in my mind, saying nothing to no one, not even to my wife. At the end of that work week, I was still thinking of a way to get away from becoming more involved in the work of God. After all, it was not as if I had neglected the work of God; I was still going to church, and I paid my tithes and offerings. What I had been asked to do was just too much.

It occurred to me that I was just attending this new church; I had not taken the right hand of fellowship. Maybe if I went to the pastor and told him I wanted to be a member of the church and become a full member, this would end my problem. I made up my mind to settle down and become a member of the church. I was going to become more involved in this church, and I wouldn't have to get out and pastor a church, which I thought the Lord wanted.

That Friday night, I went to the regular prayer meeting at the church. We sang two songs and had prayer. Just as we finished praying and sat down again, a lady, who was usually very quiet and very well self-controlled, suddenly got in the Spirit. I could see that she was trying to resist it; she did not want to cause a scene. Something was more powerful than her will, though, and before I knew what was happening she was over me, speaking in other tongues as the Spirit moved her.

She grabbed unto me and lifted me out of my seat. Holding me by the neck of my shirt, she started shaking me back and forth. Her unknown language suddenly became clear, and I could understand what she was saying.

As she shook me roughly, she said, "Go preach My gospel. Go preach My gospel." I hung my head in shame because I knew this was because of the plan I was making to keep from doing the will of the Lord. I stood guilty. When she let go of me, I just dropped into my seat, bewildered.

As I pondered over this that just took place, I heard the voice of the devil. He said, "Don't pay this any mind. This that just happened was not the Lord's doing. Everyone in this church knows that you are a pastor so this woman did this out of self. God would not do something like this." As I listened to the voice of the devil, I heard another voice say to me, "Stand up and sing this song: 'Where He may lead me, I will go. For I have learned to trust Him so. Jesus will lead me, night and day. Jesus shall lead me, all the way.'" Then the devil spoke again. "Brother Peart," he said. "Now, you know that this could not be God speaking. The pastor of the church is now speaking and you must stand and sing? This cannot be God. Remember, the Bible says that God is not the author of confusion (1 Corinthians 14:32- 33).

I quickly agreed to this. I was taught in my church that it was out of order to talk while someone was talking, so I agreed. Just then, the preacher stopped speaking and said, "Someone in the audience has something to say. Stand now and do it." I knew he was talking about me, but I was stubborn. I would not stand and sing or say what the Lord was biding me to do; I just sat with my head bowed.

After waiting a while, I could see the disappointment on the preacher's face and also hear it in his voice as he began speaking again. Oh, my God! What was happening to me? Quietly, I got up from my seat and walked out the door.

As I walked down the street, I did not want anyone to know that I was coming from church, so I took off my tie, pulled my shirt out of my pants, and loosened the neck of my shirt.

Then I heard a voice say, "Where are you going now?" This was when it occurred to me that I wasn't going anywhere in particular. I was not ready to go home, so this voice was right; where was I going? I was not in the country very long, and most of the time I was busy working, so I had no place that I wanted to go. I was just being rebellious.

As I walked, I passed by another church. I stopped and looked inside; they seemed to be having a good time. Since I really was not going anywhere in particular, what harm would be done if I went inside? After all, no one knew me in here; I had nothing to worry about. Besides, right now, I was looking like a rouge with my tie safely tucked away in my pocket, my clothes ragged, and my shirt pulled out of my pants and hanging about me. No one would know that I was a Christian, much less a pastor.

So, I walked inside and sat in the back of the church. To my surprise, as soon as I walked in, the pastor looked at me. I wondered what he was thinking. I knew that he did not know me, so why was he looking at me like that? Then the pastor said, "We will now collect our offering, and tonight I want everyone to bring your offering up here." I reached into my pocket, took out some money, and gave it to a lady that was getting up to carry her offering to the front. However, she refused to take my money and said to me with a smile, "Pastor said everyone must bring their offering up. He also said, as you bring your offering, stand in front until I send you back to your seat."

I did not want to go up there, and soon I was the only one sitting. The pastor kept looking at me. I thought it looked shameful to be the only one seated and thought about walking out. I stood up, but instead of walking out I went up with my offering in hand. I placed my offering in the offering plate that the pastor held in his hand. His eyes still on me, he said, "Everyone, go back to your seat."

As I turned to go, he said, "Not you, young man." He came right over to me. Laying his hand on me, he prayed, "Dear God, give this, Your servant, the power to go and perform Your will that You have called him to do." I was shocked out of my mind. How could he have known?

Then, he took his hand and lifted my head so I was looking straight into his face. "Brother," he said, "the Lord said I must sing this song for you: 'Where He may lead me, I will go. For I have learned to trust Him so. Jesus will lead me, night and day; Jesus will lead me, all the way. He is the truest friend to me, when I remember Calvary.'" Oh, my God! This was the same song the Lord wanted me to sing in the first church. I refused to do it and ran away from that church, trying to run from His will, but God followed me here.

"Dear Lord," I prayed, "please forgive me. I am sorry. Oh, Lord, even though I know that you can't hide from God, I have seen the proof once again." Even though I prayed and asked for forgiveness, I still felt guilty; I felt like a backslider.

The next day, I went on fasting and prayer. While praying, the Lord said, "Get up and come with Me. I will now show you where your church will start." The Spirit brought me to a spot and pointed in the direction where the church would start. While all this was happening, every now and again a feeling of doubt came over me. I felt foolish following a voice I could not see, but whenever this feeling came, the Holy Spirit would come and overshadow me, and I would burst out in worship and praise.

When I returned home, the phone rang and there was a lady at the other end of the line. "Brother Peart," she said, "there is a church in a garage started by this lady I know. She needs a pastor to take over this new work. Would you like to take a look at this place and see if you would like to be the pastor?"

I told her yes, and she told me where I should meet her. I met her and together we walked to this place. I was surprised to see that this was the same area the Spirit took me to and pointed out to me. I had nothing to say but yes. The following Sunday I was there ready for my first service. The lady went up and started the service and then introduced me to the people as the new pastor. This was how my first church in the Bronx, New York, began, and I must say the Lord was true to His Word.

Every week, the church got bigger and bigger. We started out with about ten members, but in a few weeks we had grown to twenty, and it just kept growing. Everyone was talking about the church; the worship was good, and we had some real faithful brethren. It was not long after that I felt happy that I had answered the Master's call.

In about six months, I had a strong church. We had grown to about thirty members. Then I began seeing some strange behavior from the lady who started the church; she started acting as if she wanted to be the pastor again. I watched her carefully. In about the eighth month, she came to me and said, "Pastor Peart, I need my church back."

I wasn't surprised by this. I knew she knew that I couldn't move with these people because we had no place to go, and I could not fight with her because, even though we gave most of the offering to her as rent for the place, we had no lease. So in reality, the place was hers; I would have to leave and give over to her the church that I built.

The Sunday after she made the request, I made the announcement to the members. They were upset and called for a meeting with her. We agreed that I would move in two months. In one week, I got a call from one of our members saying that they found a run-down church and the pastor was willing to rent it to us. We wasted no time; we rented this place that was already furnished. All we had to do was move in. We signed a two-year lease and moved in. Everyone who was in our previous church building moved into this new place, and the blessing continued. Souls were added to the church daily.

It was not long before our new landlord decided to move in beneath us and start up his church again. I suspected that something like this was going to happen because whenever he and his wife visited our church, you could see it their eyes and hear it in their voices that they were sorry they rented their church hall and that they wanted it back.

With our church now at about fifty members, our lease was now coming up for renewal. We were going to try to get a five-year lease this time, but before I could approach the landlord to ask for a longer lease, I received a notice, stating, "Dear Pastor Peart, please note that your lease will be up in September 1987, and it will not be renewed." I was shocked. Not again! I was not ready for this; the church was doing so well. Where in this world were we going to find a place to move to?

I called a meeting with the church, and we decided not to rent anymore; we would buy our own building. No one would ever throw us out of a building again. We left that meeting with our minds made up. We would not look for a place to rent, but we would find a place, buy it, and make a church.

We soon found an eight-family building in downtown Bronx that I decided to buy. I was sure that the Lord wanted us here for a few reasons: First, the price was right; second, it was a big building with four floors and eight apartments, and we could make the two apartments on the first floor into the church hall; thirdly, we could rent the other six apartments to help us pay our mortgage and take the pressure off the brethren. However, there were some drawbacks.

First, it was downtown, not everyone wanted to leave uptown and go downtown, and we had to find transportation for them. Second, since it was in the city, there was little parking available. Third, the area was not very safe, so vehicles could be broken into. After weighing our options, half of the church decided that they would not follow us downtown.

This was not good, so we decided that everyone would try to find a building uptown. We only had two months and two weeks, though, so I decided that if, in one month, we couldn't find another building, we would be forced to buy the building down-town. After searching for a month, we could not find another building, so we bought the building downtown.

This proved to be a challenge, but God proved that He was with us. Even though it was agreed that we had to take the build-ing with the current tenants, we didn't know how this was going to work. All we knew was that we were buying it for our church, so we put it in the hands of God; He would have to work it out. We went to closing and were surprised to find the first floor apartments completely empty; the tenants heard that a church was coming there that needed those two apartments, and they moved out before we got there. So, this was one way the Lord showed us that He was with us in this.

As soon as we bought this building, we started working on it. You will find some of the experiences of this early church hard to believe, but this will help you answer the question. Is God real or what? For example, one day, while working on the building, one young man who lived upstairs came down and started peeing in the part that we were repairing for church.

I thought this was very rude so I went and stopped him. He started cursing and swearing. He said, "We don't want any church here." As I tried to talk to him, he got angry, and threatened to get a baseball bat and beat me.

I replied, "You will be beaten with a baseball bat instead of me." He just walked away cursing. About a week later, I was inside the building when I heard an uproar outside. When the deacon and I investigated, I saw two young men holding this guy who was peeing in the church hallway, and they had him on his back and a woman standing over him, beating him with a baseball bat. Every time he was hit, he look at me with sorry in his eyes. I knew what was happening here; he promise me a beating with a baseball bat, I turn it back to him now this was pay day. The bible warns of this over and over again,' do My prophets no harm.'

Since that day, I had no more problems from him. He showed me the greatest of respect. Learn this: be careful of what you say about or do to God's children; it may come back to you.

We had heard that this building was one of the main drug spot, and soon I received a message from the drug boss saying, "You must leave this building. It belongs to us." I sent back this reply: "Forget it. We are claiming this place for the Lord, and we are making a church here. I do hope you will come one day and worship the Lord with us."

I never heard from them again, but I knew that they were around, hoping we would give up and leave. Some people were afraid that they might come and shoot us while we are having church, but I was sure God had chosen this place as a church and so His will must be done, and He would see it through.

Soon the renovation of the building was complete, and we moved in and started having church. The police department came by and thanked us for putting a church there. We promised to make a difference in this area, and we did.

After a year, the changes were evident, and after a few more years the block was one of the safest in the area. I will forever be thankful for the people of my church who helped to make this mission possible, and also to the many pastors and churches that worked with us to help establish this church in this area.

THE GREAT MISTAKE MANY PEOPLE MAKE

I have seen a great error that many of my people make in this world. To explain what I am talking about, let me take time to say that in my life, God has allowed me to meet and rub shoulders with people that are considered important in this world, and maybe as you read this book you may look at yourself as one of these people. Even as I write this, I am sitting in the home of a well-blessed woman in Ghana Africa. I am saying "well-blessed" because, after learning the story of this very prominent woman, I have come to realize that she is one of the few who has taken her wealth and blessed many people. She has opened her house to many poor and needy people.

As I met these people throughout my life, as far as I can remember I have never envied them or begrudged them for what they have. You see, in my life I have learned that some people who become rich and famous in this life do not always get their wealth honestly; many rob, kill, lie and cheat to reach where they are in life. Some have even stooped so low that they rob the poor and destitute.

You see, there are those of us who think we are here to gain the world; we do so much wickedness in this life, not remembering that we are just here for a short time. Opportunity to rob and steal and reach heights in many illegal ways have come my way, but I stayed humble and honest, and so should you.

Many years ago, one man said to me, "God is not like some father who goes around fathering children and make no preparation to take care of them; the world has plenty for everyone to have and live happy, but some people have too much. Sometimes, it's like sitting around a table with food for everyone, but as the food is passed around, some take too much, and soon, the food runs out. Some are overly full, and some are still hungry." What's going on here is greed and selfishness; we think only of ourselves, and everyone else could die as far as we are concerned

Yet, I have seen so many who live this way, but in a little while, even before they have the opportunity to enjoy all that they have spent years heaping up, they die and leave it all. Even though we see this happening, we still end up doing the same things; we never seem to learn. The Bible says in Proverbs 30:12, "There is a generation that is pure in their own eyes, and yet, is not washed from their filthiness."

Also, read Ecclesiastes 4:8, which says, "They heap up riches not knowing who will gain it." From this quotation, we see that it is not just now that we are like this, but all the way back to the time of Solomon, people have been the same. I am in no way emphasizing that we should not be rich or strive to be rich, because this is a blessing from God to you, and if you look in the Bible, you will find that most of God's people were blessed and prosperous. But remember, the Bible says "if riches increase, set not your mind on it" (Psalms 62:10).

I believe that we are blessed to bless others. For example, we have water pipes in our home—a very valuable blessing to us as we only have to turn the knob and out pours precious water. We are like a water pipe, filled with blessings. Oh, how some people long to drink of us, but we will not let off; we live only for ourselves. Have you ever seen a water pipe that has not been used for a long time? When it is finally turned on, can you see the rusty water that comes running out? That's how some people's lives are; you have it all right, but you are not giving out. You should read Matthew 25:31- 46. Does this sound like it could pertain to you? If so, in what ways?

Now, I know that things happen in life to discourage us from helping and sharing, but just try to be wise as you try to help where there seems to be a need. Even though I am a pastor, I will not deny that there are crooked people out there waiting for an opportunity to prey on you. I myself, in trying to help some who seemed to be in need, have also been ripped off by thieves who come in the name of the Lord. Let me pause here to say that, as you read this book, if you are one of those who are going around robbing and lying, you may think you got away, but the Lord is watching; you will pay one day, if not here on earth then at the Judgment. The Bible says "For we shall all appear at the judgment to give account for every deed done in your bodies, whether it be good are bad" (2 Corinthians 5:10).

I said all this to make this point: Some of us are blessed by the Lord because He wants us to bless others, but what I have seen a lot is, we get and we keep. Even though we don't need, we still take; we are not giving anything away. Consider these incidents, and see if you can find a good solution.

Mr. Brown grew up in a poor family. He struggles hard, and soon things change; he comes into some money and with good investments, and he soon goes from a poor man to a wealthy man. He has no children, so he lives only with his wife. Soon, Mr. Brown moves out of the rank of the poor because he is now rich. He does not need the poor anymore; he only needs them to work for him. He has a lot, but he gives away nothing.

One day, Mr. Brown said, "I can't live in this little house anymore," and although it was only he and his wife, decided to build himself a bigger home so as to look good in the eyes of man. The house has ten bedrooms, three baths, two kitchens, etc. Because he and his wife are selfish, they seldom have visitors, and he was not blessed with children, so there were no children in the home.

Tell me, what do you think was it necessary for him to build this big house? Well, I can hear your answer loud and clear: That's his money; he can do whatsoever he wants to do. You may be right, but let's look at another scenario. There was another man who grew up in a very poor family. The family didn't have much. For many days, they could only have tea and bread for dinner because this was all they could afford. Even though they had little, they still gave to missions a freewill offering to the poor. Soon the man of the house came into some inheritance that changed his life; he went from a poor man to a rich man. He never forgot where he was coming from, however, and he kept all his friends and was able to give even more than ever. Tell me, which of these do you think is more blessed? I hope you now see the vision; we are blessed to bless others.

If you are one of the people who find pleasure in helping others, keep up the good work; one day you might be surprised at the outcome. A few days ago, someone told me a story about how they went to look for a job at this place. After completing the application, he was called in by the boss. He wondered why, since there were three others who also had applied and they were told to leave the application on the front desk and they would receive a call.

Later, he learned that when the boss saw his name, he wanted to meet him. As he sat at his desk being questioned by this man, he wondered why he was being asked personal questions. Then the boss said to him, "I know that you may not know me, but I know most of your family. Your mother and father were good to me. It was because of their help that I was able to go to school. They fed me many times. Because of this, you are my brother, and from now on, whatever help you need of me, just ask and I will do it." There is a scripture in the Bible that says, "Cast your bread upon the water and you will find it after many days" (Ecclesiastes 11:1). Can you see how this scripture was fulfilled? Even though this man never knew that his mother and father had done such good, two complete strangers met and look at the outcome. This is one reason why I encourage doing good because you never know; it may come back to you.

As I am on this subject, I can remember a story my mother told me: Once there was this man who came to a village to live. Everyone called him Mr. "Do Good." He got this name from the people in the village because every time he met someone, he would say, "Good morning. If you do good, you do it to yourself; if you do bad, you do it to yourself." He would do and say this to everyone, so soon they called him Mr. Do Good.

Well, Mr. Do Good was a beggar, but sometimes he would give the things he received when he begged to others. Most people did not know this. Mr. Do Good did not live far from the school, and there were a girl and a boy who always stopped at Mr. Do Good's home every evening when they were coming home from school. Mr. Do Good would go to their home in the day and ask for food and when the children stopped by him on their way from school, he would give them the same thing he got from their home.

They did not know this, neither did the mother. One day, Mr. Do Good visited the children's home. The mother, who was now tired of this beggar and planned to get rid of him forever, baked him a cake with poison in it. Mr. Do Good approached the house. He said, "Good day. If you do good, you do it to yourself; if you do bad, you do it to yourself."

"Good day," said the mother. "I have a cake for you." Taking the gift, the old man said, "Thank you. If you do good, you do it to yourself; if you do bad, you do it to yourself." He took the cake and went home. That evening, as the children came home from school, they stopped at the old man's home as usual. He fed them the cake he got from their mother. They ate the cake on their way home. When they reached home, they were in great pain. Their mother became very concerned. "What have you eaten?"

"Mother," they said, "every evening when we are coming home from school, we stop by Mr. Do Good's home, and he always gives us food to eat. Today he gave us cake."

"What!" said the mother, because she knew that she gave the cake to Mr. Do Good and she knew that she had poisoned it. Now, she had poisoned her own children. When Mr. Do Good heard that the children got sick from the cake, he just said, "If you do good, you do it to yourself; if you do bad, you do it to yourself." The moral of this story is be careful what you do or what you sow, because you might reap its rewards another day.

When I was much smaller, the elders often used some sayings to bring out some real truths, some of which I didn't really understand until I grew up. For example, they would say "you can't sow peas and reap corn." What they were really saying was whatsoever you sow you will reap. Sometimes you meet some people and, no matter how hard life treats them, they are still blessed. At the same time, you meet some others and, no matter how life is good to them, they still suffer and never turn out good. Sometimes it is the seed they sow that they are now reaping. So, my good word to you is, be careful.

HOW GOD GOT MY ATTENTION AND SENT ME A MESSAGE

As you know, we all have problems sometimes, no matter how small. I had a real bad thing about me: Even though I know that when I have problem it's best to take my problems to the Lord; for some reason, this day I had problem and forgot that I had a friend in Jesus who cares and wants to help share my problems. As I drove along the street, my mind was not on my driving but was preoccupied, worrying about this problem I had. Without warning, another car overtook me and cut right back in front of me, causing me to break suddenly.

I become upset and blew my horn to warn him. Suddenly, I saw a message on his bumper sticker that read, "Give up and let God." He stayed long enough for me to get the message and he was gone. This message snapped me back into my right mind. I realized what I had been doing and prayed, "Oh God, please forgive me for leaving you out of my life and trying to solve my problem on my own. I am so sorry."

As I prayed, I felt the presence of the Holy Ghost fill my car and flow into the inner most depths of my soul. Soon, the Spirit of the Lord removed the things I was worrying about and put a song in my mind, "What a friend we have in Jesus," and even though I was not singing out loud, the song stayed with me all day and brought healing to me. Maybe if God had not intervened at the time He did, I would have gone crazy? If you ever have a problem, I hope this story will help you. The Bible says "God is a present help in the time of trouble" (Psalms 46:1).

GOD IS REAL, EVEN IN DEATH

I would like to dedicate this chapter to those of us who have lost our loved ones here on earth. I must say that in my time, I have seen many that I know pass on out of this life; some I believe to be with the Lord, others we really don't know. I will try to bring some word of comfort to you and myself, since I myself need some form of comfort.

As I sit here to write, my mind goes back to this young woman I knew. She was told that she had cancer. When she saw that there was nothing the doctors could do for her, one of her neighbors went to her and led her to the Lord. Knowing that there was not much hope anywhere else, she came to church and very soon become a very dedicated Christian. Every chance she got, she was in church, and our church, always a loving church, accepted her with much love.

Even though much prayer was offered on her behalf, she got weaker and weaker. Soon she was admitted to the hospital. One day, I went to see her. She was lying on her back with her Bible on her chest. As I entered the room, she opened her eyes. I can still see the sweet smile on her face; she looked so peaceful. Even though she was dying, she was very happy and cheerful. As I looked at her lying there, she was not only young, she was also very beautiful. In my eyes, she should not be dying. I went up to her bed and asked, "How are you?"

"Fine, Pastor," she said. "The Lord has been good." I wondered at such great courage. I spent some time with her and then said, "I am going to pray for you." I bent over her and prayed, "Oh God, my God, I thank You for life that is in Your hands.

You said in Your Words, 'but ask and it shall be given, seek and ye shall find.' Now, Lord, I am here to ask for the life of this Your daughter. I rebuke death and ask for life. Heal her, Lord; she must not die."

As I prayed, even though my eyes were closed, I could sense in my spirit that she was not happy for the way I was praying; there was no connection. So I opened my eyes to see her staring up at me with a look of disapproval on her face. I stopped praying and asked her what was wrong. She said, "Pastor, you are praying wrong. I don't want to live; I want to go be with my Lord. Pastor, you do not know it, because I have not told you everything about myself, but I am not happy with life. In this room with you here, I might appear happy to you, but I am not a happy girl. If God heals me, I have to go back to my unhappy life. Pastor, I am so happy that Jesus saved me. Now, I am on my way to meet Him. I am ready to go; I want to go."

This really put a shock in me. I changed the way I was praying and now prayed, "Lord, let Your will be done." One week later, she was gone. She wanted to be buried with her Bible on her chest, and her wish was granted. As I looked at her lying there in the casket, I knew this was not Jenny but just the frail frame that once housed her. She was not here; she was resting in paradise where the souls of the saints go to rest.

Every time I remember this young woman and how she was ready to die, I pray, "Dear Lord, help me also to be ready," for I know not when my time will come and I too will go to be with my Lord. I believe Jenny will be watching out for me.

I think that this last statement might cause some controversy, but you must remember that we are now trying to sort through this question of if God is real, and it is obvious that the more I dig for proof, the more I am coming to see that God is real. I want to believe that this truth is now appearing in the minds of some of you also. Still, I must not make the mistake of thinking that everyone who looks at these proofs is fully convinced;

some are still open to looking for more facts before coming to an agreement.

I don't see anything wrong with this; everyone has a right to his or her opinion. May I also suggest that we keep an open mind and allow the Holy Spirit to help guide us into truth? I came upon a passage in the Bible that says, "But the Comforter, which is the Holy Ghost, whom the Father will send in My name, He shall teach you all things, and bring all things to your remembrance, whatsoever I have said unto you" (St. John 14:26). This verse is saying that we can seek help from the Holy Spirit as we continue to seek for answer to this question. So, let's keep going. Is God real or what?

This next story I want to share is also very true. It happened in one of the churches I had pastored when I lived in Jamaica. In 1979, when I went to take over the church in Clarendon, I found the church with about twenty-five members, two of which were the deacons of the church. Everyone seemed to be quite genuine, and I fell in love with them right away.

One of the deacons got sick, and after everything was done to make him well again, it was quite clear that he was dying. One day, I got a call that the deacon was now at the point of death, and they wanted me to come and see him. I entered the house and, after greeting the mother and others of the house, they brought me to see the deacon. He was lying on his back, his eyes glassy as he stared out to space. I walked over to the bed and called him by name. He fixed his gaze on me. I said, "Deacon, you have spent many years as deacon to our church. Now you are getting ready to leave us. Is everything okay with you and your Lord?" He looked into my eyes, slowly shook his head, and said, "No."

I was a bit surprised at his answer, so I stayed there and ministered to him, and after praying, I asked the question again. "Deacon, is it well with your soul?" This time, he shook his head and answered, "Yes." As I stood there, I saw a bright streak of light come through the roof and down on the bed. It rested on the deacon's chest, and then he was gone. I will never forget that, as I had never seen anything like it before. Is God real or what?

Here is another story to help us see if God is real, even in death. I have been the pastor of Trinity Faith Pentecostal Church of God for many years. One of the things we offered was a free ride to church; the members just had to call and the church bus would come and get you for church or Sunday School. There was one sister who often called for the church bus to pick her up. Sometimes I was the driver, and I can remember many days, as I picked up this lady for church, seeing her husband standing by the shop, often smoking.

Sometimes, while I waited for his wife to come from upstairs, I would lean through the bus window and ask, "When will you be coming to church with me?" He would just laugh and say, "Soon, Pastor, soon." One day, his wife got very sick, and we were invited to her home to pray. Everyone gathered in the living room, including her husband. He gave his life to the Lord that night, and he started coming to church; even if he was not picked up, he would find his way to church. He was soon baptized, and he became a wonderful Christian; he was loved by everyone, and like everyone else, he become a part of the church family.

Everything seemed to be going well, until one day he was diagnosed with lung cancer. This was bad news to us; it caused deep hurt on everyone because it seemed as if we were going to lose one of our own. Strangely, however, he never seemed to be worried but always smiled and became even more dedicated to the church. He never acted like a sick man, but we all know that, unless God gave us a miracle, we would be crying soon.

Eventually, he was admitted to the hospital and we visited him often. We all knew what was happening, but he never seemed to care. On one of my visits, he greeted me with a happy smile.

"Hi, Pastor," he said and proceeded to ask how everyone was doing. "I miss being with my brethren," he said. I was waiting to hear him say something about his sickness, but he didn't. The doctor told me that he didn't have much longer to live, and I wondered why he was still happy. Did he know how close he was to death? So I asked, "Brother, do you know what is wrong with you?"

"Yes, Pastor," he said. "I know that I have cancer and I am dying. I know also that I have only a few days to go, but you see, Pastor, I have no one to blame but myself. I have been smoking since I was a young man, and even though I knew it was not good for me, I refused to stop. I am only so glad that God saved me before it was too late. I thank you, Pastor, for leading me to the Lord. Now I am looking forward to going and being with my Lord."

I was happy to see that he took it this way, but I was still feeling sorry for what was about to happen. He looked into my eyes and saw that I was not happy, so he quickly changed the subject and began telling me some old jokes he learned from Jamaica. We laughed and I prayed, and I left. I never saw him alive again; he was gone, but this just man left an impression on my mind forever.

This other story may not appear that nice, but it may prove that there is a hell to shun and a Heaven to gain. One of my classmates told me that he and his family never believed in God until they witnessed his mother dying. His family never went to church all their life, and he never prayed because he had no reason to.

Since he was a child, he was taught by his parents that there was no God, and all those talks he heard at school about God was not true; there was no heaven, no hell, and no God. Then his mom got very sick and, when all treatments failed they were called in to say good-bye. As he approached the door, he was sad and surprised to see his mother kicking and screaming, "The everlasting pit! The everlasting pit! Not a hitch to put my foot!"

As she screamed this over and over, he stood there, surprised at her words. He had lived his childhood thinking that there was nothing to fear, but now, standing here, watching his mother die, he started thinking that there must be something he had overlooked. He watched her until she stopped screaming and fighting. Confused, he walked out of the house to the street.

As he walked pass a church, he heard the preacher preaching for the first time in his life. He walked into the church, and when the altar call was made, he walked up to the altar and gave his heart to the Lord. He is now a powerful preacher. His testimony is: "All my life I was told that there was no God. I believed it until I met the Lord. Oh, how much I have missed. I have now proven that there is really a God, and He now lives in my heart."

My next story hit me closer to home and even now, as I try to tell it, it is bringing me pain. But I must tell it; it may bring healing to someone. This is about the death of my only son. The Lord was very good to us. As I mentioned before, after our marriage, God blessed us with a fine son, and we named him Richard St. Albin Peart. He grew up to be a fine young man, and he helped to bring happiness into our lives.

His three sisters adored him. Even though, as the older and bigger brother, he was often rough with them, he loved and cared for them. He was a basketball player and invited me to watch him play, but I was often too busy and, besides, I was not a great fan of basketball. "Dad," he said, "one day, you all are going to see me on TV playing my game." In my mind, I felt it was all right to have big dreams.

He gave his heart to the Lord, and I baptized him. He stayed in the church and was our bass guitar player in the church. He was very good at this and was very dedicated. At the age of twenty-two, he came to me. "Dad, oh Daddy!" he was panting. I could see the glow in his eyes. "The greatest thing happened to me! There is this very beautiful girl who, from the first time I saw her, I fell in love with her. Today, I spoke to her and told her how I felt, and she confessed that she had been watching me too, and she felt the same way about me. Dad, she consented to be my friend."

"Okay, son," I said. "Only please, be careful. Whenever you need my help, please let me know." He giggled happily. That was one thing: my children and I got along well, and they could come to me anytime; I always would find time to listen to them. Soon, my son and his girlfriend were engaged and everyone seemed happy. However, our church had very strict rules.

For example, we did not allow sex before marriage, and to help prevent this from happening, we did not allow tender kissing, fondling, or any such things that could lead to lusting. We believed in keeping pure until your wedding day. So, one day, my son came to me and said, "Daddy, I am getting myself in trouble. Whenever I see this girl, I go out of control. She does things to me that make my head spin. Dad, if I am going to stay saved, I have to get married."

"Are you sure?" I asked.

"Yes, Dad. I love this girl and she loves me. What does it matter if we wait for five years? I am still going to marry her. So, if I do it today, it's the same."

"But marriage takes planning."

"No, Dad; we don't have to have a big wedding. All we need is love."

"Richard, do you realize that you are our only son, and if you are going to do something so important, you should make it so that we can invite our friends?"

"Father, do you want us to commit sin? I want to get married so my girlfriend and I can keep from falling into sin."

"Okay," I said. "Whenever you are ready." Within a week, he was back.

"My girlfriend and I talked, and we decided to get marry in two months."

"But that's too fast," I protested.

"Dad," he said. "remember, I came to you and you said whenever I am ready? Well, I spoke to this girl's family, and they all agreed, so we want to get this over with so we can get on with our life." So, the plan was set, and when the date came, they met me in the church hall and I married them.

Everything seemed to be going well. We would sometimes have our father and son talk, and if he asked my advice on a subject, I would try to give my best advice, bearing in mind that this was not only my son, but this was now a married man and he needed to be faithful to his dear wife. I had a big house at the time, so they were given the downstairs apartment to live in. I was happy about this arrangement; we could live as one happy family because his wife was a nice girl and we loved her. My wife and I saw her as our own child, and we wished them only happiness.

One day, my son came to me. "Father, he said. "My wife is not happy."

"Why?" I asked.

"You see, Dad, before I met my wife, I had a lot of friends. She now wants me to give them all up."

"What kind of friends?" I asked.

"Just social," he replied. Then he continued: "Dad, I know I am a married man. I know I have to be faithful to my wife. Remember, I am also a Christian. So I am not going to do any thing against the will of God. Dad, sometimes we have big quarrels and even fight. If I go out and stay late, when I get home, she will ask angrily, 'Where are you coming from?' If I say, 'I was with my friends', then it's trouble. I don't want to tell lies, so I have to say where I am coming from."

"Richard," I said, "remember, it's two of you living together. When you are not home, she is all alone; she must feel lonely. Why not take her with you whenever you are going out? You see, you do not want her to think you don't want her to know your friends. Remember, she is your best friend."

"Sometimes I ask her to come with me and she refuses."

"Well, I think you might have to change your plans and spend more time with her. Your marriage is more important."

"So what should I do? Should I give up all my friends?"

"No. We all need friends. We dare not live alone; you need to have friends, but don't put them before your wife. She also needs friends so that she doesn't have a boring life. Do you want me to come to your house and talk to you both?"

"No, Dad."

"Then, do you want me to send someone else, since you may not feel comfortable having your father speaking to you both?"

"No, Dad. I think I know what I must do. I will give up the friends she doesn't want me to keep and spend more time with her."

"I think that's wise. When I married your mother, I had the same problem, and I allowed her to pick my friends. If I had a friend she did not like, I would try and drop them so most of my friends she approved of. So do as you feel." He never discussed this subject with me anymore. I had a feeling that things were not well, but I did not want to interfere unless I was called.

One day, I was working at one of my other houses when my phone rang. It was my wife complaining how Richard was having a fight with his wife, and when she stepped in, he got upset and stormed out. She was confused because he had never acted this way before. Not long after that, I was outside working on my car when I saw him coming.

When he approached me, he was upset, or maybe I should say very confused. I had never seen my son in this state before. He kept repeating "I've messed up, Daddy, I have messed up." As he spoke, tears were streaming down his face.

"Calm down," I said. "Calm down and tell me what's the matter."

"I was rude to Mom and my wife," he said through his tears. He explained to me what he had done, and I said, "This is not death; just say 'I am sorry.'"

"My wife said she does not want anymore apologies from me because I always go back on my promises, but I tried, Dad, I tried."

"Well," I replied. "We are only human, so don't stop trying." He walked away and went under the pear tree in our yard. I saw him lift his head up to the sky and say, "Father God, please take me out of this world. I am tired of this world. Everything I try fails. I want to leave this world. Please, God, take me." I was surprised at this. Nothing prepared me for this.

Without thinking, I shouted at him, "Boy, what are you saying? Surely things can't be that bad."

"But, Dad, I am serious about this. I want to go."

"Be careful what you ask for, Son, because it might just come."

As I said, my son was a basketball player, and, as he has promised, one day I was watching TV, and there he was playing ball on the TV. I was proud of his achievements. That night, laying on my bed, I thought about all I had done for my boy. I gave him money and food, I paid for his schooling, and on one of his birthdays, my wife and I took him to the car lot and let him choose the car of his choice.

However, as I lay there on my bed, looking over the many events of my life, I found that I had missed one important aspect in his life: He needed to spend quality time with his father. So, I decided to change. I was going to finish the things I had planned, and then I would start spending more time with my children. However, I was about to find out that we do not know what tomorrow holds for us.

The Sunday after we had this conversation, we all went to church. Richard played the bass guitar, and everything seemed normal. However, something was very wrong. We tried really hard to boost the service so that we could all feel better, but no matter how much we tried, it was as if something was wrong. We just could not place our finger on it.

After the service, everyone went home. As I entered my house, I saw my son sitting on a corner of the couch. I went and sat in the chair opposite from him. Before I could say anything, he stood up and went to his apartment. I learned that he was doing the cooking that day, so he went to feed his wife.

My wife had to go to work, so it was my wife's sister who prepared dinner and called me to the table, and I went and had dinner. Suddenly, we heard an uproar outside. There were fire trucks, ambulances, and police cars in my yard! There seemed to be some emergency. I went to see what was going on. They were at my son's door knocking, but they there was no response. I very politely asked, "Can I help you?"

"We just received an emergency call from here," they replied.

"Not here." I thought that if something was wrong downstairs, I would have known. After waiting a while with still no response, I offered to take them through the house. When we got downstairs, my son was lying on the floor unconscious with his wife sitting on the bed crying. She started to explain that they were having dinner together and he just collapsed on the floor. The emergency crew jump into action and tried to revive his heart, which stopped unexpectedly. After repeated tries, they thought they had a pulse, and took him to the hospital. He was taken to the ICU unit, and we started praying for his life.

We spent night and day at the hospital, hoping for a sign of life. The power of God was so rich in the ICU ward that all the sick in this area got well and left; only my son was left there. The doctor confirmed that he was brain dead due to lack of oxygen to his brain and told us that there was little hope he would survive.

Then my mind went back to his request under the pear tree: "Take me, Lord. I want to leave this world." Could it be that his prayer was now being answered? No, I could not accept this. This is my only son; surely God would not take away our only son from us. I just could not give him up. Prayer was being offered everywhere, and I, with my family and the church, would not let go. So, Richard stayed in this state.

Eventually, many people in the church began receiving visions and messages from the Lord that they all interpreted to mean we needed to let go, but this was hard to do. I went to have a talk with the Lord; I wanted to talk with Him. "Dear God," I prayed, "what are You doing to us? Have I not served You faithfully most of my life? Why do You want to take my only son from me?" I prayed and begged.

Then the Lord spoke to me. He said, "Curtis, for many years now in your ministry you have seen the death of many a people, both young and old. Don't you think pastors' children die too?"

To tell the truth, I had not thought of this before, but now that it was brought to my attention, I took time to think of this. However, even then, I still did not want to give up my only son, and so I went back right to my complaining. God then sent someone to comfort me because everyone was worried because when the pastor has a problem, everyone has a problem.

So this brother came to me and said, "Pastor, last night I had a dream. I dreamed that I was searching for Richard. As I searched, I came to this river. The water was so pretty and calm. There was a man who seemed to watch over the river. He was also the keeper of the boat to cross over to the other side.

"I walked up to him and asked, 'Sir, have you seen Richard?' 'Yes,' he said. 'He already crossed over to the other side.'

"'Sir,' I said. 'Will you give me a boat that I might go and get him?' 'No,' he said. 'Leave him alone. He already crossed over and he is all right.'

"Then I woke out of my sleep, and as I pondered over the dream, the understanding came: The days for Richard on this earth are over; even though they have him on life-support system in the hospital he is already gone."

Even after I got this message from this brother, I still had hope, and when the doctors told us it was all over, we asked for him to stay connected to the machine much longer. We prayed and prayed, hoping for a miracle, but one more day passed and still nothing happened. The family finally came to accept that he was gone, so at last we prayed, "Lord, let Thy will be done." Within an hour, it was all over; Richard was dead.

When someone passes on without consciousness, it causes you to worry and ask questions. Even though I knew that he was saved, and even that the day when he went into unconsciousness he had just came from church and was even on fasting, I still worry, and I hope to meet him one day when my life in this world is over. I cannot even fully express how I felt. I remember I had such a funny sensation. One thing that kept my family going was the fact that all things were in the hands of our Almighty God.

After the funeral, I unwittingly went into depression. I did not want to go on with life anymore. What's the use? My only son was dead. It took a lot of prayer and seeking the will of God to bring me back to myself. If you are one of those who have suffered the death of a loved-one, and maybe even now you are hurting, may you take a few words of comfort from the Bible (John14:1, John 14:18, John 16:33, Psalms 38:9, Psalms 63:1, Isaiah 25:8, 1 Corinthians 15:54).

This other story found in 2 Kings 13:21 is also a very wonderful scripture, showing how great the power of God is, even in death. Read it; this will inspire you. When we lose our loved ones, we feel like it's all over, like we will never see them again. In a little while, I will show you in the Bible how happy our loved ones are if they die in Christ, but first let's look at the story of the dead body of Elisha in more detail.

According to the Bible, Elisha was a man filled with the Spirit and power of God. One day he died and was buried. The Moabites had now invaded the land and were robbing, killing, and making many into slaves. One day, some of the Israelites were burying a man in the same area where Elisha was buried.

They saw a group of Moabite men coming and, fearing them, they let down the dead man's body into Elisha's grave.

When the body touched the bones of Elisha, who seemed to have been dead for a long time as he was decaying, the man woke up. Even though Elisha had been died a long time, the power of God was still in his bones! Oh, glory to our great God!

Now, let's look at what happens to our loved ones after death. According to the Bible, remember this only applies if you died a follower of Christ, He promised that where He is, there shall we be also (John 14:3). The Bible teaches that there is a place called paradise where the dead in Christ go after they part out of this life. It is a place of rest (Hebrews 4:1, Hebrews 4:9).

I know my next few words on this matter may seem too hard to swallow by some, but I still will say them. I believe the word of God, which says that if anyone is sick, let him call for the elders of the church who will pray, anointing with oil, and the prayer of faith will save the sick, and if they commit any sins, it shall be forgiven (James 5:14). St. Matthew 9:12 also says that if you are sick, seek a physician. The Bible also says ask and it shall be given, seek and you shall find, knock and it shall open unto you (Matthew 7:7). It also says, "And if you will ask anything in My name, I will do it" (John 15:7). Yes, all this I believe with all my heart, but I also believe where it says, "It's appointed unto man once to die, but after this comes the Judgment" (Hebrews 9:27).

Yes, my friends, death is an appointment to every man; it doesn't matter how we try, we must face death some day. If this was not so, then the rich man would be able to buy life and not die, doctors and scientists who would do anything to prevent death would do so and not die, but death is a reality for every man. We can only be ready because we know not when or how it will come.

This leads me to something I am aching to say, not biblical, but just a personal thought. You don't have to believe it; like I said, it's just a personal thought. I believe that every person that is born into this world is here for a set time and, when we were made, we were made with many different parts. Just as motor vehicles are made up with many different parts, so are we.

Depending on the make of the vehicles and the mind or intentions of the maker, one is guaranteed for one week, another for one year, and another five years, and so on; it is all up to the maker's discretion. The vehicles cannot ask, "Master, why did you make my mate live for forty years and I for two?" He is the master, and he does as he sees fit. With this, I believe that when the limited time given to each particular vehicle is coming to an end, different parts begins to fail, and if you really want this vehicle to live longer, you have to change the defective parts. Sometimes this works, other times it does not because as soon as you fix one thing, another part goes bad. Sometimes it's better to put it away.

Look at me, for example. I have a car that I love because of its quality; I could not buy a new one, so I bought it used. It was getting old, but it looked good, and every time I got in it and drove down the road, I felt rich and important. Soon, the engine failed. When I told my wife what it would cost to fix the engine, she said, "You better get rid of this car." After thinking about it, I decided to fix it, so I spent some money and fixed it.

After a month, the transmission went, and again my wife told me to get rid of the car, but I decided that I already spent too much on it. If I put it away now, I would lose, so I fixed it. Six months went by, and it needed body work. This I did. Now, after all this I have a car that is now twenty years old, and I am still trying to hold on to it because I eventually spent so much on it to keep it alive. I have to face reality, though; it is dying. Such is man; no matter how we try to stay alive, we are dying. It's the law of life.

Let's look at this: Suppose death should lose its power and no one died anymore, but children are still being born into the world. Have you ever thought about what would happen after five years or so? Also, suppose God should answer all our prayers to abolish death and bring back all our loved ones to life. What do you think would happen when they come back for their homes? There wouldn't be room for everyone. I am saying all this to point out that death must happen, and God is not being wicked when He allows a loved one to pass on.

Solomon said, "The whole duty of man is to serve God and keep His commandment" (Ecclesiastes 12:13). I am speaking to myself as well. Sometimes when the time for our loved one to die comes, we will not let go and we get angry with God. Let's change our attitude; I am not saying you are not to mourn, but in the time of your grief, look back and thank God for the time He has allowed this flower in our lives that helped to brighten up our days.

Before leaving this story, let's get some comfort from the Bible (1 Corinthians 2:9-10, Psalms 94:12-14 and 91:9-15, Psalms 23, and Romans 8:18:39). According to the Bible, we shall have joy, peace, happiness, and God shall wipe away all tears from our eyes (Revelations 7:3-17). We are promised a mansion where Christ lives (St. John 14:1-3). The Bible also teaches that death will not hinder us (1Thessalonians 4:13-18), and that if we died in Christ we shall have rest (Revelations 14:13). The Bible also teaches that to get to heaven, we must be changed out of this body and God shall give us a new body (1 Corinthians 15:50-58). I do hope as you read these scriptures you will find comfort. I hope the sorrow in your heart will turn to gladness; know that our loved ones in Christ are not gone forever, but we shall meet them again someday.

A VISION
OF HEAVEN

One night, I had a vision of heaven. I remember as a young child I read and heard so much talk about a place called heaven. The stories were so fascinating that I often longed for the time to come when I would go to live in that city, a city where all is peace and rest.

Then one night I had a dream. I dreamed that I was on a long, tiresome journey, but for some reason I knew that I had to keep traveling; I knew that I should not stop for anything. Some of the paths I traveled were dangerous and frightening, but I remember telling myself I had to keep on traveling.

On my journey, I met some friends who wanted me to turn and go with them, but I said no; I must keep going. I took time to invite some of them to go with me, but they all refused, so I ended up going alone. I passed places of pleasure and felt the need to stop for a short while to get something to eat and maybe enjoy myself a little, but then my journey seemed much too urgent to stop; I must hurry, so off I ran. I went down hills, up hills, and through valleys. Then it occurred to me that I was traveling to heaven. Suddenly, I felt happy and hurried on.

I came upon a steep hill that was too steep for me. I stumbled and slipped, and I had to get on my hands and my knees, but I couldn't stop now; I had to make it over this hill. I also realized that I was alone on this journey—no one to talk to, and no one to help. This was so discouraging, but the thought of heaven kept me going. As I climbed higher and higher, I got tired and I began thinking of the life I left behind, my friends, my family, the trials, the good times and bad times. Yes, I had now left this all behind and I was on my way to a new country.

After much struggle, I finally reached the top. I then turned around and looked at the path I had traveled and how far I had come. Praise God, I had finally gotten over the hill and now I was standing on top of this mountain. I turned to look at where I was going. In the distance, I saw a city. Its beauty was too much to explain.

It was full of light, or rather, the city itself was pure, bright, clear light, such light that I had never seen before. It shone clear and bright. Everything around it shone. I stood for a while to admire this city, and then I started to run down the hill and across the plains, keeping the city in my view at all times.

As I got closer, I saw the golden gate to the city. I was happy; I had finally made it home. I walked up to the gate. It was made of gold. I lay my hands on the gate, but before I could open and walk in, I woke out of my sleep. I was so disappointed. I went back to sleep, hoping to pick up where I left off, but I was unable to go back to sleep. For the rest of the night, I laid there and thought about the dream I just had. Oh, how I wanted to enter this city!

The next day, I told my dream to my mother. With a sweet smile, she said, "Your spirit was traveling. If you had opened the gate and gone in, maybe you would have died; you would not have come back to us." These words from my mother made me think if I would rather go or come back. I concluded that I would rather go to be with my Lord that night.

HOW CLOSE AM I TO THE LORD IN THESE LAST DAYS?

Before I answer this question, let me first explain that I am human and apt to failure, just as any of you. I have my days of ups and downs, but even if I fail in some of my ways as I try to live a holy life unto the Lord, I never stayed away from my Lord for too long, because I know that I can't make it on my own.

In 1 John 2:1 it says "My little children, these things write I unto you that you sin not. And if any man sin, we have an advocate with the Father, Jesus Christ the righteous." Verse two says "And He is our propitiation for our sins: and not for ours only, but also for the sins of the whole world."

As Phillip said to the Ethiopian, understandeth what thou readeth? I will try to use the word *advocate* to explain what the Bible is saying. Here, this word means a go-between, to stand up for. An advocate is a person who pleads on your behalf if you should be in trouble. For example, in court, the person who pleads for you, let's say your lawyer, would be your advocate. Similarly, after the death and resurrection of our Lord, the Bible says Jesus is now before the Father making intercessions for us (Romans 8:34). So, if we sin before we drop dead, Jesus will plead to the Father for us.

I said all this to explain that I have never considered myself to be perfect, but I long to be. I know that God is real; I have proven

Him to be real and now I stand to bear witness that this God we serve is real.

As you may remember, I gave my heart to the Lord at the age of nine. I am now fifty-five years old and find no fault with the Lord. In fact, I am even much closer to Him now than in my early years; now we have a much closer relationship. In my early years, my contact with the Lord was mostly in church, in my prayers, or through visions or dreams (my favorite), but today I know that the Lord is with me because I feel His presence all around me. I know that the Holy Spirit is real because I feel the anointing on me, especially when I have to preach His Words.

I said I felt His presence around me. This is one experience I wish you all could have. Most times, when I am alone, even driving in the car, the Spirit of the Lord comes and fills the place or the car. Then we have sweet communion. We talk together, person to person. I ask questions and He would answer. He asks questions and I would answer.

I can remember one day when I went on a long journey. The Spirit of the Lord came and joined me. As we traveled, we talked like true friends would. I felt so blessed to have Him accompanying me. I prayed for this to continue forever. It was such a sweet, perfect feeling, it made my body quake and tremble in His presence.

When He speaks, it seems to go straight through me. You could try this too. I know that there are many of you readers who can testify to this and who have also witnessed the same. However, if you are out there, you know the Lord but have never experienced His presence in this way or in others ways, such as in church or maybe while reading the Bible, then you need to. You will not have a real testimony of God's existence until you have a personal contact with Him. You say you know Him, so talk to Him and let Him answer. Seek and you will find.

The joy I feel when I am in the presence of the Lord cannot be compared with anything I know. To feel His touch, hear Him whisper, "I love you," to experience His great work in your life is the best. If you have not experienced this, what are you going to testify about? We speak of the things we know, and by this I mean that we must have our own experiences in the Lord so that we can tell others of what we know.

The Bible says that Jesus wanted to know what His followers thought of Him, so He asked, "What do men say about me?" So they said to Him, "Some say You are John the Baptist; some say You are Elijah; others say You are Jeremiah or one of the Prophets."

Then He said to them, "Who do you say that I am?" Jesus expects us to know Him for ourselves, and I believe that if you want to testify about someone, you need to know the person and not just believe what someone told you.

Believers today need to adapt something from the cow. After the cow eats the grass, it finds a shaded area, lays down, and brings up the food it had just eaten, chewing it over and over again. In my country, we say the cow "chews its cod." This is how it should be when we read or hear the word of God; we should pray and make sure of it before we swallow it.

As I answer the question of how close am I to the Lord in these last days, let me tell you of God's presence on my third missions trip to Ghana, Africa. I was called to this mission field in a way I can hardly explain. As I climbed the steps to the plane, I realized that I was heading to a strange land, so I questioned myself and the Lord as to what I was doing and where I was going. I do not enjoy plane rides, and I enjoyed even less getting on one and traveling for such a long journey. As I questioned the Lord why, what, where, and how, the only answer I received was, "Don't worry; you will find out in time."

Well, I had a very successful trip and was able to accomplish some great feats for the Lord. I was able to observe the way the villagers lived and how it differed from the city people. The women seemed happy with their ordinary lives living in their mud huts and raising their children. Their church seemed to be a very important part of their lives. The village people also seemed very loving; I remember as we were about to visit one village, we came to the base of a mountain. The guide pointed to this high mountain and said, "We will be going up that mountain."

I asked, "Are you sure the car can make it?" He said it could. We were a bit overloaded, though, because we had picked up a pastor, who was our guide to this village.

As we proceed up the mountain, everything was going well when we suddenly came upon a truck that was having problems climbing the hill. We came up behind it, and our driver had to shift down to a lower gear. This caused too much pressure on our car, but there was nothing we could do.

The road was too narrow, making it impossible to try and overtake the truck, so we had to stay behind the truck as it crawled up the hill. It was not long before our car got overheated and our radiator exploded. We had to pull off to the side of the road. There was smoke coming from under the hood. We got out quickly, since we did not know what would happen when we opened the hood. Then it occurred to me that we were stuck in a strange place very far from home; it was not a good idea to let nightfall catch us there.

As we stood there wondering what to do, I started to pray. Yes, it was time to seek help from the Most High. I stepped aside and whispered a prayer to the Lord. Then the driver said he thought he could fix it, but he had to go back into town. He hailed a taxi and went back. While he was gone, I cleaned the spot and made it ready. In about one hour he was back, and we were able to repair it. Thanks be to God, it worked, and we were soon on our way up the mountain. We reach the village, accomplished what we went to do, and got back home late in the night.

My journey to Ghana was successful, and I was now very happy that I had made the trip. I now clearly saw why the Lord needed me to go to Africa. I also pledged whatever the Lord needed of me, wherever He sent me, I would go. St. Matthew 28:19 says, "Go therefore and make disciples of all nations." Isaiah 6:8 also says, "I heard the voice of the Lord saying, 'Whom shall I send, and who will go for us?' Then said I, 'Here am I; send me.'" It gives me joy when I am able to fulfill this command. Someone has to do it, and I am so happy God has chosen me. The way the Lord works in my life, both when I am home and in other lands, helps to answer the question is God real or what? I do hope that as you read you too will be able to answer this question.

I think I am much closer to the Lord than I have ever been before. As you will see in my stories, I still have sweet experiences with the Lord. When I call Him, He is there and He is full of surprises; He causes unexpected things to happen in my life, things that He knows I will be in need of. I am not saying that He always provides everything I need, because there are times when I need help and I call, but He seems nowhere to be found. I do not fully understand the ways of the Lord, just as many of you out there. Sometimes I find that the things I think I could not live without I did not really need at all. Because of this, it's only fair to say God knows best; it's best to leave things in His hand and let Him do what He knows best.

GOD PROVED THAT HE WAS WITH ME ON MY MISSION TRIP

I spent ten days in Ghana, and it was time to head home to America. I had no idea that this return trip would prove to be so amazing; the Lord proved to me that He was with me and confirmed this through miracles. I am about to tell of some unbelievable things that happened on this trip. If you find them hard to believe, I cannot blame you, because if someone told me these stories, I think I too would have my doubts as well. Everything I share here, however, is the truth.

As I prepared to leave, I said good-bye to my friends, and we set off for the airport. Even though there was much traffic on the street, we got there on time, so I did not have to wait long to be on my way back home to America. As I went to the check-in counter, I said to myself that I should ask for a seat where I would be able to stretch out my legs because I had much pain in my legs.

However, I decided against asking and told myself whichever seat I was assigned would be fine; I would sit there and try to make myself comfortable. I didn't pray to the Lord about this; I only spoke of my wishes in my mind. (Remember I said before that we must be careful what we say in our minds, because God is a reader of minds, and He doesn't have to hear a word from our mouth to answer our prayers.)

I boarded the aircraft and found my seat, 15F. I placed my carry-on in the overhead compartment and sat down. But something was not quite right today. Suddenly I was overcome with a great fear and a voice in my head saying, "You will not make it home; this plane is going to fall out of the sky and everyone will die."

I recognized this voice; this was the devil paying me a visit. I can't say why I listened, but this brought great fear on me. Just then, I heard the voice of the Lord speaking to me, "Have no fear. All will be well. Behold, I will be with you always." Although I know that this was God and his words are true, I said, "Prove it, Lord."

It was a full flight, and everyone settled in their seats and prepared for takeoff. I also settled in. I could see that I may not enjoy this flight home, because I have long legs, and my knees was already touching the seat before me; then, once more, I said in my mind, *Why did I not ask for a change of seat when I had the chance? The only thing that could happen is them saying no.* Then I saw the flight attendant coming down the aisle. She came straight to me, looking past the guy who was sitting beside me. She asked, "Sir, would you like me to change your seat for a seat by the exit with more leg room?" I was a bit surprised to see that she came to me, passing all the others who would be happy for this opportunity, but I quickly said, "Yes," and was escorted to a seat that was by the exit.

The lady who was sitting there wanted to give it up, as she was not happy sitting by the exit. Now, I could stretch out my legs. Isn't God real? This was great! I needed a window seat and I got it; I needed a place to stretch out my legs and I got it. I was very happy to know that the Lord was watching out for me, but I had to be sure. So, once more, I asked for more signs that He is with me.

When it came time for snacks, the flight attendant came down the aisle serving drinks. She stopped at each row and asked what they wanted, then she would take a glass, put some ice in it, and pour the requested drink. Some people asked for juice, some asked for water, some asked for coke, and so on. She would do the same thing for each person's request. As she approached me, I said in my mind, "I need a full can of drink." Soon, she came to me. "I will have coke," I replied.

She took a glass and started adding the ice as she had done to everyone else, even to the man sitting beside me. I was thinking that I wouldn't mind having the whole can of coke, but I wouldn't dare say this to her. It would not look good, seeing that everyone, as far as I could see, only received some drink in a glass. I would appear greedy and selfish.

However, as soon as I said this in my mind, the flight attendant took up a can of coke and was about to open and pour it into the glass, but then stopped, handed me the glass with ice and a full can of coke and a pack of peanuts. I took it and said, "Thank you."

As she started to move away from my seat, in my mind, I said that I would like another pack of peanuts. Suddenly, she turned back, looked at me as if to say, "Why didn't you ask me?" and handed me another pack of peanuts. So here I was, sitting in my seat, the only one with a full can of drink and two packs of peanuts. How does this look to you? By this, I knew that the Lord was with me on my trip, and He knew what I needed by reading my mind. You may look at this as a mere coincidence, but I know it was the favor of the Lord. He said in St. Matthew 28:20, "And I will be with you always, even to the end of the world." This may seem simple to others, but to me this was proof that He was with me on this trip. So with my mind at ease and my fear removed, I settle down for a great ride home. Isn't God real.

Let me share some other miracles with you. I have a lot of debts. My monthly bills add up to about $3,000 per month, but my monthly income is only $2,400. I should have very bad credit. On the contrary, though, I have very good credit. You might say that my wife helps with her income, but she has her own bills; we own a vacation home, and she is responsible for all the bills it accumulates. Also, I cannot touch her money, so I have to pay the bills somehow.

So what do I do? I trust God who is the Good Father and wants His children to trust in him. The Bible says, "Trust in the Lord with all your heart and lean not to your own understanding" (Proverbs 3:5). Let's look at other scriptures that will help fully answer the question of, is God real or what? In Psalms 23:1, it says "The Lord is my shepherd I shall not want," and in verse six, "Surely goodness and mercy shall follow me all the days of my life." Luke 17:6 also says, "If you have faith as a mustard seed you can say to this mulberry tree, Be pulled up from the root and be planted in the sea and it shall be done."

Similarly, Matthew 21:22 says, "And all things whatever you ask in prayer believing, you will receive," and Matthew 7:7 says, "Ask and it shall be given to you, seek and you will find, knock and it will be open to you." St. John 14:14 states , "If you ask any thing in My name I will do it," and Ephesians 3:20 says, "Now to Him who is able to do exceedingly abundantly above all that we ask are think."

All these and much more cause me to trust God more. When I start to feel the pressures of life, the word of God, the memory of how God came through for me in other times, the stories told by others of the greatness of the Lord, I just trust in God with all my heart; He has proven to be a God of His words.

One day, I was about to pay my bills and found that I did not have enough money. I wrote the bills and sent them off. As I mailed them, I prayed, "Father, I sent these bills off and trust You to take care of this." I felt relieved now that I had given it all to the Lord; I did not know how the Lord would deal with this, but I left it up to Him. To my surprise, I checked my bank account a week later and found that no one had cashed the checks that

I mailed. Not only that, but things stayed the same until money was there to pay the bills.

There was another time when I sent off checks to pay the bills. I knew that my Lord could take care of it, so I committed this to him. Then, my wife checked the bank account and said to me, "There is money in the bank that we did not put there." She wanted to know if I had put more money in. "No," I said.

"Well, there is three thousand more dollars in our account than what we put there." We went to the bank to report that there was a mistake made in our account, but after checking, they told us that they found no mistake and the money was ours. We gave thanks to God for watching out for us.

After about a week, the bank contacted us saying that someone mistakenly put some money in our account and they would have to withdraw it. That was okay, because by then our bills were already taken care of and money was there for them to take. The Lord had sent me help from unexpected source, unbeknownst to me, and after a while it became the norm.

While I did the work of God, He took care of my every need. One day I was concerned about how my bills were going to be met. I heard a voice say to me, "Leave it alone; you do not need to know everything. Finding out may weaken your faith. All you need to know is that your needs are being taken care of." So this time I obeyed the voice and left it alone, but it was still on my mind. I needed to make a budget.

So one day, I took my pen and paper and sat down and made out a budget. I put down how much I made and how much I paid out monthly. I soon found out that I was spending out more than I was receiving, but after I did this budget, I felt guilty. I knew why I shouldn't have disobeyed the still, small voice that was saying leave this alone. After this, I started getting bounced checks; my account started having a negative balance, so I had to go back to the Lord and say I was sorry for disobeying His voice.

After a week, I forced myself to forget what I had learned about my finances and, after a while, things went back to normal. To this day, I am still trusting the Lord to see that my bills are paid, and He never fails. Not only that, but whatever I need, I only have to think of it, and it would be taken care of. You see, with such happenings this makes God so real to me.

After laboring as a pastor in New York for about fourteen years at the same spot in the Bronx, we soon realized that we needed a bigger building to accommodate our growing church. We decided to start looking around. There was a building for sale at 1109 Burke Avenue in the north Bronx that we passed all the time but never tried to buy because we concluded that we could not afford such a property.

After all, we only had $25,000 and, based on the location of this building and the size of the land around it, we knew it was beyond our reach. We decided this without even checking it out. Yes, my friends, we can hinder our blessing by thinking too small. Be warned.

Anyway, one day I was talking to my brother, Paul, who is also a pastor. I said to him, "We have outgrown our church and we are praying and searching for a good spot for our church. We are so desperate that we will take whatever we find, if it's even an old broken-down building, as long as it has place for parking and is in a good location."

Then he raised his eyebrows, and said, "Haven't you seen a building on Burke Avenue that has be up for sale for some time now and no one seems to want it? I understand that that building was a supermarket and it has been burnt out for five years now."

I looked at him, and with a chuckle I said, "That building? Yes, I pass it almost every day, but I don't think I can afford such a building. Just by looking at it, it seems expensive, and I don't think I want to trouble anything we can't afford."

"What are you talking about?" he said, "Anything that is for sale can be bought."

"Yes," I said. "But we need money."

"Don't worry about that. Go and check out the building." I listened and immediately went and copied the telephone number off the for sale sign. I called and made an appointment to see the inside of the building on the day of the inspection. It was a sight that would discourage anyone, but I decided to take it and was given a price of $500,000. After discussing it with the church board, we decided to make an offer of $430,000 but settled on $450,000.

I was told that we had to pay all this money in full, and no bank was willing to lend this money, because the building was in bad shape. Where were we going to find this money in such a short space of time? We only had $25,000 in hand.

The sellers waited patiently for me to call, but I just could not call. Where would I get this money? If I had more time, then maybe we could raise about $300,000 by refinancing the building where the church was now, but it was too little time. Besides, even if we made up $300,000, where would we get the rest of the money? We needed $400,000 plus $10,000 for closing. The sellers waited for us to call and come in and sign a contract of sale, but how could we?

One day, I got disturbing news that one owner of a hardware store went and made an offer. He told them that he had the cash in hand. To this day I do not know for sure how much he offered, but I know that this was truth; he did make an offer. When I got the news, I was disappointed. I really needed this place for the Lord, but it is not good to be poor. Tuesday night was prayer meeting night, and I told the brethren of the bad news; we were going to lose the property to someone who had the money to pay cash.

Someone got up and addressed the group. "We need this building. That man may have the money, but we have the Lord." We all agreed, and so we formed a circle in the middle of the church, held hands, and prayed. We placed this in the hands of the Lord, believing that even though it seemed to be a lost battle, the Lord would do something.

After a week, I received a call from the broker. He said, "Hi, Mr. Peart. What happened? I have been waiting for your call." I was quiet. What could I say?

"What happened?" he asked. "Did you change your mind? Do you still want the place?"

"Yes we do." I became quiet again.

"What happened? You don't have the money?" Before I could answer, he said, "The owner will carry the mortgage." This was good news to me. I said, "Thank you. I will come tomorrow and sign the contract. I understand that the contract is with my lawyer?"

"Yes," he said. "But if we are going to hold the mortgage, I will have to make a new contract. I will fax a new one to your lawyer. I will call you when I do so, and you can go and sign it."

"Okay," I said. We did not delay; as soon as we got the call, we went and signed the contract and paid our earnest money. We left the rest in the hands of God. While waiting on everything to be approved, I had a meeting with the church, and it was decided that we would refinance the current church building, so this was what we did. Within thirty days, we were ready with over $270,000. This was how we come to own one of the most beautiful spots in the Bronx as our church location. It seemed impossible, but now it came through.

After buying the building, we had some very hard work to do, but we were thankful to God for such a blessing. After about three months of owning the building, I went into a hardware store and soon learned that the owner of the hardware store was the same man who offered cash for the building. I know this because we started talking, and he confessed to me that he was the one who offered cash for this building.

Then he said, "Tell me something; I have been wondering about this. Which fool could have something for sale, was offered cash for it, but refused it? Tell me, Mr. Peart, how you pulled it off. I offered cash for the building. You asked for a mortgage; they refused my offer and accepted yours. I can't understand this."

"Sir," I replied. "This is not man's doing but God's. You trust in your money, we trust in the Lord, and God never loses."

And so, my sisters and brothers, if you have something to do and it seems to be impossible, give it to the Lord; He never, ever fails. I am saying this because in my life I have seen pastors who want to buy a building for the Lord's work but are afraid of entering into something they think they cannot manage.

I do hope my testimony will encourage you to do what you know you have to do to bring through the will of God. He needs someone to work through, and that may be you. I don't know or understand everything about God, but as I live from day to day I am surely learning, and even when I think I learned all I need to know, I see new things. We will never be able to know everything about our Lord.

GOD—OUR PRESENT HELP IN TIME OF TROUBLE

I remember I was sick, had to stay in bed, and my payment in the bank was due. To pay this bill, I had to go to the bank and make the payment, but because of the way I felt I dared not get out of bed. I could have asked my wife to do this for me, but there was no money to give her for the payment. As I worried about this, I remembered that I had a rich father. I turned my eyes and mind to him and prayed, "Father, today is the last day for paying this bill. I am sick; will You see to this for me?" Then, I just left it to Him and relaxed my mind. You see, I had confidence that He would take care of it.

I felt better in three days and went to the bank to make sure all was well. As the clerk looked at my payment record, she said all was well. Surprised to hear this, I asked about the tenth of June. I was sick and was unable to come and make payment. She looked again and said that was also paid. I said that it couldn't be paid because that day I was sick in bed.

She then showed the record to me. "See?" she said. "Someone came and paid at 11:30 in the morning. I remembered that was the same time I asked the Lord to pay the bill for me, and He did. I turned to her and said, "Now I remember; I asked Daddy to come and make payment for me." Is God real or what?

Another example of how real God is: I pastor a church that was blessed with a lot of young people. One of the young men in this church got into an altercation with someone who did not attend the church and cut him with a knife. This young man was arrested for his crime; normally when someone gets into the type of trouble he did, a member of the church board would go with that person to court. Now, because we know that he was in the wrong, we are praying for him, but what shall we do if he even had some right? When he lost his temper and cut this man, he became wrong.

When his court dates came, I decided to attend with him since I was indeed his pastor. The church continued to pray for him but didn't really know what to pray about. How could we pray for his freedom when he was in the wrong? We prayed for God's mercy to fall on him.

I went to the court and sat in the back. I listened as all different cases were called up and dealt with. As far as I could see, this was a rough judge, and he seemed to pardon no one. Once more, I bowed my head and prayed. Then, after three weeks of constant prayer, finally the Lord answered. "What do you want Me to do?" He asked. I answered the Lord by saying "confuse the judges," knowing that if the judge was confused he could not fairly pass judgment on his case.

A little while later the case was called up, and the two men stood before the judge. He asked them what happened. As they spoke back and forth, the whole thing sounded so confusing. Suddenly the judge said, "Stop, stop. I am confused," and the law said that when the judge is confused, he cannot pass judgment.

Then he said to them, "You both go home and behave yourselves. Court dismissed." Even though this was what I asked for, I was surprised at how the exact thing I asked for happened. Tell me, is God real or what? Have you come up with a conclusion? I have.

On Wednesday 15, 2010, I walked into my house and proceeded to check my mail. I came across a bill from the City of New York, which stated I had an overdue bill that needed to be paid immediately or my property would have a judgment against it. The notice went on to explain what a judgment on my property could mean and how it could affect my credit.

After going over this bill, I realized how serious this could be for me. I had been doing all I could in these hard times, trying to keep up with my bills. Now, out of the blue I was faced with a bill I could not pay. The only thing I knew to do was lift this bill up to God and pray for help.

"God, here is a bill I cannot pay. Please pay this for me." I put the bill down, walked away, and didn't give it a second thought. I learned that once you give something to the Lord, you need to leave it with Him. Two weeks later I received a reply from the city. It stated "thank you for your full payment of this bill." To this day I don't know how God did it but I give Him all the praise for paying this bill in full.

In summary, we see that our great God is interested in the way we live, the food we eat, our social and mental health, and our saved and unsaved life. Isn't it good we have a God who loves and cares for us? I am not saying that God is going to deal with everyone's situation the same way He dealt with mine, but I am happy He revealed Himself that way to me.

In the Bible, we read of a dear friend of Jesus who, like me, wanted proof that Jesus was the Promised one to come. He sent his followers to Jesus and asked, "Are you the Christ or do we look for another?" (Matthew 11: 2-3). Now read Jesus's reply in verse 4-7 of the same chapter. Not everything you ask for you are going to receive. Some people ask and receive, while others may ask and never receive. All things are in the hands of the Almighty God. He will deal with things as He sees fit.

CONCLUSION

I have always known that there is a God. After the many times that He has revealed Himself to me and sent me help, how could I ever think less? But this question is one that I have heard many times. Some even go as far as to say, "If there is a God, then let Him show Himself."

Others have said, "If there is a God, then why this or why that, but I must testify that God is good. So, let's not walk around and act like there is no God. Know this: If you need a friend, seek one before it's too late.